THE BEST SERVANT STORY:
LIFE OF TONY ROAM

God Knows Best

Antonio Garcia

Gotham Books

30 N Gould St.
Ste. 20820, Sheridan, WY 82801
https://gothambooksinc.com/

Phone: 1 (307) 464-7800

© 2023 *Antonio Garcia*. All rights reserved.

No part of this book may be reproduced, stored in a retrieval system, or transmitted by any means without the written permission of the author.

Published by Gotham Books (November 21, 2023)

ISBN: 979-8-88775-604-2 (H)
ISBN: 979-8-88775-602-8 (P)
ISBN: 979-8-88775-603-5 (E)

Because of the dynamic nature of the Internet, any web addresses or links contained in this book may have changed since publication and may no longer be valid.

The views expressed in this work are solely those of the author and do not necessarily reflect the views of the publisher, and the publisher hereby disclaims any responsibility for them.

Table of Content

Introduction iv
Chapter One 1
Chapter Two 7
Chapter Three... 16
Chapter Four... 27
Chapter Five 37
Chapter Six 45
Chapter Seven... 56
Chapter Eight 62
Chapter Nine 65
Chapter Ten 73
Chapter Eleven 77
Chapter Twelve... 81
Chapter Thirteen 89

INTRODUCTION

The focus of this book is on gang life. It is about the second chance I got in life, going on to become one of God's Best Servants. When I first thought of what to call my book, I knew, "Best Servant". I pondered over such lofty words. What did they mean? About whom was He speaking? I want you to realize that I am a faithful servant of God, who now understands my talents and purpose in life with the help and guidance of the Holy Spirit of God. I am no longer timid to share all that I am and hope to be but I am persistent and motivated.

It had been years since the Holy Spirit covered me like warm butter on a porous slice of bread, entering me.

As I was driving down the long stretch of Main Street of Georgia, I was having thoughts about things I wanted to write about. I saw THE BEST SERVANT STORY as a revelation from God.

I pray to God, "Could that mean a name for a book?" and "Is it referring to the Holy Spirit?" or, maybe, "Is it something you want me to preach about?"

Have you ever had something come to you, knowing it is God ministering to you, but you can't put your finger on what it all meant? I figured out, eventually, that it was God's choice for the title of my book. It took some convincing on God's part. It would be thirteen more years before I finally picked up the pen.

This book is about the Holy Spirit service to the chosen people of God. Yes, it is about me, but it is also about you, too. It is for those who desire to increase their level of understanding about God, and those who have begun to thirst after Him daily, who want to serve Him with all their being. It is you and I, who will P.R.A.Y.: Praise, repent, ask, and yield. It is you and I who will become two of God's best servants, by B.E.S.T.: Believing, evangelizing, serving, and testifying of the Kingdom of God

It's also about the angels that surround new believers, and those who were protected by them until they were saved. I was chosen to be ordained for a calling from Our Lord God Almighty. How I struggled to express that I Antonio Garcia (Tony Roam) was God's child. I was adopted into His family. I want to be one of His best servants, and hope that you will, too.

I started the book with a few longhand words on some notebook paper. With such primitive means, I grappled through a few pages. I stopped as soon as I got discouraged because I lost my apartment. After settling into my next living arrangement, I began writing again, but soon quit, again, when I lost my job and everything and didn't have a place to stay. Have you ever known what God wanted you to do, but you found one obstacle after another in front of you?

Certainly, discouragingly, I was about to throw in the towel when I lost my notebook! But Spirit kept urging me to keep on going. I knew I had to obey Him. I was eager to be immersed in His Word, but to write about it was uncomfortably like hard labor.

I fervently began fasting and praying, asking for a sense of direction.

I didn't know how to write proper sentences. To make this book come to life was a major challenge. I also have a speech impediment; A bit of a lisp when I say "s" and Epilepsy as a child. Those things held me back for quite some time. Then, after I had gotten very close to God, I let my weaknesses down. I dropped them into a bottomless hole. I took up the cross and never let go. You should hear me preach a sermon now and how great I have become as a writer.

I am His Trustee, so to speak; His executor of His Will. Scripture references are from the King James Version. May you not just enjoy this book, but also take it to heart.

Because, if you have a desire to make sense of life, as I had, then you will find that the Holy Spirit and the Word can clarify it and lead you. Preachers and Pastors can be Spirit filled, and all day matters of life to make you GOD's vessel.

CHAPTER ONE

Boundaries

The first thing I saw in my first cell was a cement floor that had a puddle on it. The second thing was the cot, which was also wet. My eyes filled with tears.

Waiting for my day of release from prison, I learned many scripture verses. had been in long enough to get a pattern going. It took me about three weeks to figure out when to speak, when to shut up, when to wake- when to shut up- when to eat- when to shut up.

Lights were out soon. I tried to get comfortable so that sleep would come. But the cot was hard and kept my thoughts alive. I put down my Bible, and began to think about my childhood.

When I was about nine years old, my mother took us to Puerto Rico. She was in love with a man named Victor, who also had a big family there. Victor wanted my mother to meet them. She was terrified of flying, but she took every cent she had saved, and boarded a plane.

We didn't leave much behind in America. We first lived in the Puerto Rican community of Hartford, Connecticut. This was a place where lives were typically born, lived, and lost within the same neighborhood.

We stayed with Victor's family for a few weeks, then traveled over to Gurabo to see Aunts and Uncles, and all of mamma's cousins. We didn't come back to the United

States for three more years, and only went back to the areas we were familiar with; New Jersey and Connecticut.

We arrived back in New Jersey first. It was similar to Puerto Rico. The poverty, the hungry dogs roaming the streets, the bodega, (a Spanish word for corner store), and the street peddlers selling their wares were familiar sites. We kept our Puerto Rican traditions, like parades and quinceañeras and quinceañeras (a special party for sixteenth birthdays).

But the schools in America were crowded, and the teachers had no time for you. In our district, teachers were barely educated themselves. The streets were lined with trash. The milk was never fresh, and the people dressed alike. How drab the streets were! I thought about the graffiti on the walls as a touch of life.

I could never catch up with the children academically who were also born here in the United States, but spoke English at home. Mamma spoke only Spanish to us, so she had no idea how to help us with our homework.

Victor was working hard at his jobs all day. He would come home so tired at night and crawl into bed with mamma. But before he did that, he would reach over and turn the picture of my mamma and my real papa upside down.

My mother grew up in the peaceful town of Caguas. She had a small baby there, but no husband.

That is where she met my father, Daniel Garcia, a fine looking man, who wore his hair like Elvis Presley. He wanted to marry her, and become the father of her baby boy, Luis, needed, and he was happy to have such a beautiful young lady in love with him.

Looking for work, mamma and papa settled in New York with Luis, found minimum wage jobs, and began their own family. That is around the time that my earthly life began,

10/15/1970, being born to Daniel Garcia and his wife, my mother, Marta Garcia (Marta means bitter or provoking). I was a skinny, frail-looking boy, with rich dark brown eyes and a wide grin. Before I was born, my brothers Luis Danny and Ralf were born. That made four boys, all close in age to each other, for mamma to raise single-handedly. My father left right after I was out of diapers.

When papa was gone, there were plenty of suitors who wanted to step in and take care of my mamma. Mamma was attractive, with long shiny black hair and intense brown eyes. Her flawless skin had a radiant olive complexion. It didn't take long for Victor to enter our lives. The Victor family and my big family merged, with some marrying into the other ones' families.

When I first got locked up, I had been sure that I would wake up at any moment: that this was a play I was dreaming that I was in. The cot was really something my buddies put there as a prank for me, and the Correction Officers were the stage managers. But how could I explain the rest of the sights I saw? - The cells, one after another, in long rows and stacked until there were several different floors of them?

I was dreaming all of it. It just **had** to be a dream. It HAD to be a **DREAM.** Through a lot of obstacles. He waited patiently for me to knock on His.

But it wasn't a dream at all. God's plan of salvation was being revealed. I know God has covered me with His love and protection door. When I faced things truthfully, I grew in wisdom. But that didn't happen right away.

What was it like to know you were going to prison? It was preparation mixed with trepidation. It was regret ringing with retaliation. It also made me count every blessing that I ever took for granted!

Now I can look back with such gratitude for all God has done for me all my life. I can now marvel about the fact that God had chosen me long before I ever chose Him. When I was three years old I went to a parade with my uncle, who had permission to take me. Uncle Felipe was always trying to entertain me when he babysat me. Look at the girl dressed like snow white! Look at that baton twirler! So, as we sat watching the parade, on a windowsill seat built for two, four stories high, we laughed and watched the commotion below. My uncle didn't know I had fallen until, splat! I hit the ground and by the mercy of GOD later on I heard I fell on my 2 feet from the fourth floor. It was that fast. One minute I was snuggled up on the corner of his elbow, and the next second I had plummeted into the middle of the parade.

My mother has told me that it was my father who took me to the hospital. Papa was not living with us at the time, but he heard that we were going to be up in the window of Aunt Maria's apartment.

Papa had gone to the annual parade with his girlfriend to watch the parade, and to look up and watch me. He watched me, in the hospital, too. He watched and waited, until there was word from the doctors that I wasn't going to die or be paralyzed. Then, and only then, did he tell my mother. Mamma also told me when papa died. It was only a few months later.

"No, you can't tell me that!" I screamed. I was four years old and asking for my dad. "Where is papa? I want my papa!" Over and over, between my sobs, mamma told me he was dead. But she was not going to convince me of that. NEVER.

When I was about six years old, I asked about my father everywhere that I met someone new. It didn't dawn on me to only seek out the ones who had been in my community since I was a little child.

Someone thought he died in a casino. Someone said it was right in our own neighborhood pool hall. Someone else said, no, he died at the hospital up the street. Someone said he thought my dad never even made it to a hospital.

Some thought he could have had a heart problem. But no one really knew for sure. They hadn't cared to talk about anything but their own problems and their drugs.

"What did you say? He died?" asked one stoned man. "What did he die from, boy?"

Looking back, I saw that it was my father, I was *sure* of it, who asked God to spare me and use me for His glory. Some say God saved me from that fall so that I would be able to preach about Jesus Christ the son of GOD. Some say I was saved from death so that I could serve others. How I wished that I was able to do that. Just let me out, and I would do that. I would make papa proud of me. I remembered looking for my papa for about four years. As I grew, I continued to ask for my papa, searching relentlessly. Walking the narrow streets lined with shabby brick apartments that once had been very stately, I was determined. "Do you know who my dad was? Do you know who Daniel Garcia was?"

Some of them remembered him, but no one could say what had happened to him. As my days turned into years, I finally gave up and accepted that he was gone forever. He was gone, but I hadn't known if I made him go, or if it was something else.

During this time, new people came into my life because of my openness to talk to strangers. God has a reason for planting people in your life. There were always some lessons to be learned from each one.

Occasionally, street evangelists would come to our neighborhood. They fed soup to the hungry and wanted the people to say a prayer with them. I didn't understand what those people were praying for. I understood that they had a Bible. I didn't know much more than that, as a small child. But, I did know that I needed my rosary for prayer time. I never saw them with one, ever. They offered me a Bible, but, at that time, I refused.

Some of the scripture verses I read my first year in prison: Numbers 11:17 says, "I will come down and talk with thee: and I will take of the spirit which is upon thee, and I will put it upon them; and they shall bear the burden of the people with thee, that thou bear it not alone."

1 Corinthians 2:12 says, "Now we have received, not the spirit of the world, but the spirit which is of God: that we might know the things that are freely given to us by God."

Acts 17: 24-25 says, "God that made the world and all things therein, seeing that He is Lord of heaven and earth, dwelleth not in temples made with hands. Neither is worshiped with men's hands, as though he needed anything, seeing he giveth to all life and breath and all things."

Psalm 37:17 says "For the arms of the wicked shall be broken, but the Lord upholdeth the righteous."

CHAPTER TWO

God Finds You

I was only allowed to shower for five minutes twice a week. A corrections officer would watch me the whole time. It was amazing that I even had time for thoughts during that short time, but I had thoughts that terrified me.

After my shower, I was led back to my cell. I thought about fear and what the Bible tells us about it.

Sure, I had visions and dreams, and real scary nightmares with Epilepsy. They come often as children. But these fears were not like those as a child.

I remembered telling my mother about my bad dreams, when Epilepsy but never about the good ones. I wanted her utmost attention and sympathy. I was a small boy, who had felt lost in the shuffle of life.

I thought about dreams in school when I was supposed to be doing my work. I thought about angels standing by me when I had trouble in school. And, I had lots of trouble in school.

When I came home from school one day, when we were freshly back in the United States, I told my mother about the bullies in class. She shrugged her shoulders and rang the palms of her hands together. "Oh, Dios mio," she would say. But she couldn't do anything.

I don't know what I expected her to do, but I expected her to do SOMETHING!

I could only work out the frustration by fighting against my brothers. The wrestling got real rough at times. I was told not to be a crybaby. So, I would continue to charge after them.

I saw what happened to kids who would not fight. I thought I needed to hurry and get bigger. It was a struggle to gain weight, but I tried to eat as much as I could.

When I was weighed at the doctor's office at the age of 10, I was less than 65 pounds. Mamma was concerned about my thinness, and always offered me extra portions of food.

I went from being a gaunt scarecrow to a not-so -much but - still gaunt scarecrow. One of the biggest gangs around was recruiting my friends, and I had wished to join when I was strong enough for them to accept me. I practiced kicks and punches all day long.

I had to quit thinking about my childhood fast, or I would get tears in my eyes. Mamma taught me to always have hope. Yet, I was losing hope.

I couldn't leave the cell. Twenty-two hours locked down, all you have is lots of opportunities to think. I remember when I first walk in Morgan County Jail, In Hartford and a inmate says to me, I know you are not going believe this, but I serve Satan, ass a young man for many years and seen lots of magic and witchcraft is a lot better to serve the true GOD for Satan deceives people and those words have always stay in my heart. I knew there was something different when he said to me I want to give my life to Jesus Christ and stop this life I have lived for many years.

I opened my Bible that rested across my chest. I had been given the King James version, and had no idea that there were easier to understand versions.

God made the WORLD. He made everything. He dwells in the temple, not made with human hands, but in human hearts. He does not need what you have in your hands, in your cupboards, computers, or in your wallets, as though He needs anything. He needed nothing, and I needed so much to truly find Jesus Christ.

I was awaiting trial. I had a Bible now, and I had found another Bible in one of the cells that they moved me to after going from one jail cell to another at times waking up with Epilepsy attacks in the cell but not knowing what happened, because you don't remember the compulsion or what happened. Thank GOD, for the Bible at times was left there by the last inmate that had my bunk. It is the book most often requested in prison, and the book that is most often left behind, as well the most important book in our lives to protect us and give us wisdom.

I had my rosary around my neck, and rubbed it as I opened my Bible. I tried to figure out what the scriptures meant, and how they pertained to me.

I was reading the writings of the Apostle Paul. I surmised that Paul was saying to the people that they were not serving the correct God. I was Catholic when I was locked up. I was aware of God - but did not know Him. It wasn't because I was Catholic that I wasn't close to God. It was simply that an awakening of the knowledge of how real God was hadn't yet transpired being always in my life through everything.

I recalled being scorned by a bully for being Catholic, an older girl who wanted to pick on me. She said I was stupid for being Catholic. She made fun of the priest and the nuns.

I had asked mamma why we were Catholic, and she said that Puerto Ricans have been predominantly Catholic for a very long time.

I didn't care who was and wasn't a Catholic, at seven and eight years old, I just wanted to hold another hand. As an inquisitive child, I got to know many of the people in the community. Some were predestined by God as Sunday school teachers, and some of them read me stories of the true patriarchs in the Bible. The dictionary I used said that a patriarch was one who was the head of a family or tribal line. It was a person regarded as a father or founder of an order or class. Moses and Jacob were patriarchs. I was sure that my father must have been a patriarch.

Street savvy people taught me some lessons, too. They taught me how to count change, how to dribble a basketball, and how to wear black socks so that they don't show the dirt.

They tried to get my mind off papa. They tried, but it never worked.

As I lay on the cot that had a thousand stories of its own, I thought about all that, and I thought about papa. I remembered one person telling my family that papa died too young. I was young. I was one of the youngest inmates in this prison. I had thought, could that mean I would die soon? I remember now having to Epilepsy attacks that really scare me, one in North Avenue in Bridgeport County Jail that I was in the top bunk and I saw my self leave my body, and the second one was I wake up in different cell and don't know what happen just that Correctional Officer says you need be by yourself in the cell. I wanted people to look up to me, and didn't want them to fear me anymore. But, I sure didn't want to get killed in there, either. Let me tell I had a few fights, let me remind you safety is important, as I was going through this whole prison sentence, always as a child have had Epilepsy attacks and found out at the age 43, the day my wife found me in the bathroom ice cold ready to die that GOD was always here. Never, knew this GOD was always by my side the Spirit was always protecting me and serving my cause to this world. I believe like Paul Silas and Peter in prison I knew when it was time to protect myself even when I was unconscious with Epilepsy attacks the Holy Spirit served me like I have always had the help of GOD. Amen

My sentences could have been longer if my behavior wasn't perfect. It would be a difficult act to show that I wasn't going to be pushed around, yet not get in any fights with other inmates. I remember being move from cell to cell and at times not knowing why, I believe the Epilepsy at times will trigger of and people being afraid of me, I had times guys will ask for me to be move, to another cell and I will wake up different moods at times, didn't want to wake up or very angry.

I got in trouble mainly because I was in one of the many gangs that lived in Hartford, Connecticut. There were several gangs in Hartford, and I was a member of one when I was twelve, then another when I was fourteen.

There were several other gangs, such as gangs in other cities. For the most part, people would look at our gang like we were just a bunch of troublemakers, and that is what we were. There were a few older guys out on the streets that talked to us. One of them was Ice. Ice was my good friend, who wore a size twelve shoe at the age of fourteen. He was a very kind, soft - spoken boy.

Black Jack, his dad, lived with his brother and his brother's family. He didn't look down at us, he liked us, and so he gave us drugs.

The other adults that talked to us were street people. You could tell who they were, by the kind of clothes they wore, and by money they didn't have... Except for one lady. She wore new shoes and had a fancy purse across her arm. She talked to me as if she understood and cared for me.

Then, one day, she told me she knew my daddy. She had known who I was, from the first day we talked. I told her my name when she asked for it.

"Antonio Garcia," I told her. Her eyebrows raised. She looked me up and down, but I didn't know why. She realized who I was. She could see that I looked like my dad.

So, after a couple of weeks, this lady who was dressed too nicely to have been living on the streets, told me that she knew papa.

"Your daddy was killed, you know," she said, matter-of-factly.

"He was shot in the back."

"No, I didn't know," I answered.

"Yes, he was. It was a case of mistaken identity. The man the shooter was after looked just like your daddy. You see, it was a different man altogether that the killer wanted dead, but your daddy, he, well, he looked like that man, and … you know …" she trailed off. She was mentioning something about the man who was supposed to have been the target being a Puerto Rican, too.

I had known deep down he was dead, but murdered? Shot in cold blood? My face must have had a horrified look on it, because she apologized several times as she scurried away. That night, and several nights after that, I had dreams of my father getting shot in the back.

I was too old to do it anymore, but I wanted to run into my mother's bedroom and tell her that I was having a bad dream, that I had found out papa was dead, and it was torturing me. Only I didn't go to her. Because I was a tough guy, a big boy of twelve years old.

The Bible says that I have been known by God since I was in my mother's womb. In the comfort emanating from her chest, I used to feel more than love. I had felt Godliness in mama's arms. It was the same feeling that I have now, when I think about God's love.

I recall, on the first visit from mamma, asking her if she had gone to the annual Puerto Rican Day parade. She said she had. We talked about small, insignificant subjects that would escape my mind as soon as they touched the air. I got around to asking her what was concerning me.

"Mamma, what is wrong with that lawyer you got?" I asked. "They are going to make decisions with or without him. Where has he been?"

"He is Tony's new attorney Tony, he never had a case like this before," she replied. "I told him a week ago that he was supposed to get to work."

When I asked her to get someone who knew what they were doing, she shook her head.

"Baby, you know mamma doesn't have that kind of money," she apologized. She was working at a factory that was little more than a sweatshop.

Don't think my mamma was one of those parents who refused to acknowledge the wrongdoings of their young. I don't believe she was ever like that. But I begged her to believe that I was innocent, and she did.

If she would have had money for a better lawyer, she would have given it out in the first place. Mamma lived that motto of giving of yourself for your child, even if you have nothing else to give them.

Mamma told me that it would work out.

"Please don't worry, Antonio (Tony Roam) ," she would always say.

13

She had hired a lawyer that was new in the business, and would take payments. When she found out what he was like, she fired him and took up a collection from the whole family for a better lawyer.

Prison is a rock bottom. When you first arrive, you think that you will never again ever do anything that will ever possibly land you back in. Then you see all the repeat offenders, and doubt your own resolve.

A friend told me once, that we often find the greatest spiritual leaders to have been destitute bundles of sorrow at one time in their lives. She said that God kissed their pain away, and now serves Him just as if they had never had any cloud filled days.

I was humbled by God -so that He could lift me up again. After only a short time there, I saw many inmates who were repeat offenders. The fact was, I was scared that I would return to the streets, too.

Mamma was happy to see me study God's Word, but neither of us was aware that someday I would become one of God's best servants.

I end this chapter with an image of a small boy, so small that he looks twelve instead of sixteen. He is standing in a line of prisoners. He is naked. He is going to be asked to bend over and cough, so that they can make sure he has nothing up his rectum. That small boy was me to be for GOD Rey Bendecido Pastor/ Artist / Author / Investor.

Other scriptures I read in my first year included the following:

Isaiah 41:10 says, "So do not fear, for I am with you; do not be dismayed, for I am your God. I will strengthen you and help you; I will uphold you with my righteous right hand."

Ephesians 6:12 says, "For we do not wrestle against flesh and blood but against principalities, against powers, against the rulers of darkness of this world, against spiritual wickedness in high places."

Philippians 4:8 says, "Finally, brethren, whatsoever things are true, whatsoever things are honest, whatsoever things are just, whatsoever things are pure, whatsoever things are lovely, whatsoever things are of good report; if there be any virtue, and if there be any praise, think on these things."

Revelation 14:13 says, "And I heard a voice from heaven saying unto me, Write, Blessed are the dead which die in the Lord from henceforth: Yea, saith the Spirit, that they may rest from their labors; and their works do follow them."

CHAPTER THREE

Screaming and Kicking

Locked up in Bridgeport, Connecticut, God was talking to me about new things. He reminded me that I was spared for His purpose. The guards would have had me for supper, if they had known what I was accused of. It was in the newspaper, so it was just a matter of time...

A group of them did find out, eventually I got into fights and people heard about Antonio Garcia (Tony Roam) street name. At the next location I was transferred to, three of them grabbed me by the arms and legs and threw me on the floor.

They ambushed me when I was supposed to go for a visit in the beginning visitation room. I never made it to mamma's visit that day. I fought as hard as I could to protect myself, and they gave up before they were able to break any of my bones. God protected me.

God speaks to us in our quiet times, and, confined, I certainly had a lot of those. Quiet times can be torture, but they have a purpose. They served God's purpose.

My search for God didn't start because I was looking for something to believe in, though most do it that way. For me, it was a matter of being in the exact spot that God wanted me to be in... helpless, broken, and ready to jump out of my own skin and into something great, something powerful and convincing.

It was not because the judge lashed out at me in the courtroom. It was not the degradation that prison inflicted upon me. Nor was it the bright blue jumpsuit we all wore to look like convicts - from a VERY long distance.

I closed my eyes on my bunk and thought about home. But, *which* home would fill my thoughts this time?

Maybe the constant moving about caused my childhood memories to be cloudy. Bits and pieces came to mind as I recalled each place we lived in.

My mamma and Joseph lived together as husband and wife, traveling together from New Jersey to Puerto Rico, and back again, until I was twelve, when we moved to Connecticut. They moved us often from apartment to apartment, so I did not have a stable environment. In the first year back to America, we moved twice.

There is a vicious cycle of poverty and crime. Where you find poverty, you will also find crime. Every new place attested to that fact. There were often screams and gunshots echoing outside at night and gangs fighting all over the place hustling and selling drugs.....Park Street little Puerto Rico.....

Two adults and four children did not fit well into a one bedroom apartment. We all knew why we had to pack ourselves in. Victor, didn't have to explain that we were dirt poor. His killing our pet donkey in Puerto Rico emphasized that fact.

It was shortly after moving back that I started having nightmares. I remember having many that made me so frozen with fear that I couldn't move or scream. Epilepsy seizures are very scary and the body paralyzed as you go into amnesia you can't remember anything. Upon waking, or a few moments later, I could move my arms again. I would slip out of bed and climb.

I went into bed next to mamma and didn't remember anything, just scratches and bumps and my body hurting a little. I never needed to feel afraid in my Aunt Tia's house, back in Puerto Rico. How I missed Puerto Rico! I remember my laughter as I ran across those white sandy beaches. I remember my astonishment to discover the loud, bird-like sound of the coqui in the rainforest. I remember the love my classmates showed me when I skinned my knee. I loved that rooster that my stepfather turned into a fighter, and made us eat on Thanksgiving Day. I had a bunch of relatives in New Jersey. And, later, I found out that I did have a huge family in Connecticut, too. That gave me some sense of home.

It didn't matter that Victor was sleeping next to mamma, I wanted to be in the bed next to her.

One night, mamma had enough of me getting in her bed. She told me that nine-year-olds don't do that…

I was certain she hated me. Only an hour or so earlier, she had yelled at me. We were all sitting in the living room, watching TV.

"**Antonio**! GET OUT! GET OUT OF THIS ROOM! GET TO BED!" Mamma shouted. "I am sick of you ruining the movie we are all trying to watch. And you ruined the whole movie, now, didn't you?"

She was referring to the very plausible endings that the movie could have, and that I told them my prediction of how it would end. I always did that. Most of the time, I was right.

She sent me back to my own bed. Oh, I knew, then, she didn't love me. She loved Ralf. It was still etched in my mind; an answer to the question someone asked her about which child was her favorite.

"Marta, which one of your boys is your favorite?" her cousin asked.

"Ralf," was mamma's quick response. I heard it plain as day. I was standing in the shadows, and my whole body stiffened. I was no longer interested in playing with the kids at the party. I wished I could run away.

That next summer I asked to stay at a relative's house. After getting shuffled off to two other relatives' houses, I decided to come back home. I called mamma and asked her to come and get me. She and Victor came and took me back home.

So, I was back in Hartford, being forced to go to school in worn out hand-me-downs. I skipped school to look for papa once or twice, but I went most of the time.

I was in a new school, called Sixteen, in New Jersey. There was fighting like I had never seen before. Even the kids that liked you were mean to you.

I learned how to behave by watching others. I recall one wintry day when I was playing outside with the children in the snow. I pushed the little girl my mother had been babysitting, and she fell a bit harder than I expected her to fall.

Loud wailing erupted. This upset my mother, which in turn upset my brother Danny, who in turn, beat me up. I didn't know how to tell them that I liked her, I really, really LIKED her, and that is why I pushed her. I daydreamed often about that girl, yet, to this day, I cannot recall her name.

Oh, people had loved the little kid who was always saying the meanest things! The first words you learned from those neighborhood children were swear words. My mother and uncle and all my cousins could not see my behavior as anything CLOSE to adorable.

And I was screaming in my sleep. My cries at night about visions of angels finally scared mamma enough to drag me to a psychologist's office. She told them that I was belligerent and seemed to be oblivious to her voice. I was defiant in that office room, too, because, as the lady continued to ask me question after question after question, I kept playing with the toys on the floor. She put them there for children to play with, so why would she bother me during my playtime?

"Antonio, "Antonio, "Tony," my mother would repeat. But I would run and do whatever I wanted to do. My siblings didn't bother to play with me much, and I didn't mind. I liked playing all alone.

Or, if I could see that someone was trying to make a bed, or cook a meal, or do anything that seemed like they could use some help with, I was right there grabbing a pillow, or a bowl, or whatever it was they were working on. I wanted to help.

More than one family member said to me, "Why do you want to help? Don't help, because you always do it wrong," Sticking out my tongue, I would get a mean temperament. It was better to get nasty back at them than to let them see me cry. I wasn't a crybaby. I knew I was a helpful boy, mamma had said so. It didn't discourage me from trying to help others. It just made me more persistent.

I was frustrated as a child. I had no clue about what true frustrating situations were like when I was only nine. "Danny, you go help out with fixing the porch, your uncle is trying to get some new boards on it," mamma said, one day. Danny was talented and smart and could fix things. Sticking my arms out at my mother, I would beg her to look at how strong I had become. **I** could fix the porch. See my muscles? She shrugged me away and told me to go to work on my dancing or something. I ran and got the radio. The salsa music channel was mama's favorite channel. I would sway back and forth in front of mamma. She said that I was artistically inclined. She rocked back and forth in her chair, smiling brightly at me. I enjoyed her watching me. I swooped and swayed and bowed and spun. Dancing and singing were so much fun!

The school year ended, and we moved a few miles away. Once again, I had no friends. I liked my brother Ralf's friends. Though they were only a year older than I, they wouldn't consider me a playmate. I found friends of my own – friends that Ralf's didn't approve of.

Oh, how mamma wished that I was still a small child, not brave enough to go out alone - still staying close to home. But I did get out, and way too much. Sometimes, she would call me through the window of the third-floor apartment. I would just wave my hands and shake my head, telling her that I wasn't coming in.

I especially liked Ralf's girlfriends, and they seemed to enjoy my company. The following year we moved again. This time, it was not only a few blocks away. It was to Hartford, Connecticut.

The teachers at schools in Hartford sometimes confused me. We were so close in age that some thought we were twins. Ralf's and I were the best of brothers, very close and we were also nine months apart. Some people said I looked like my father. Ralf was also getting that from people.

People would yell for Ralf when they saw me walking down the street. That was such a compliment to me, because he was very special in my eyes.

My brother, Danny, became *especially* important to me the winter when he almost died.

We had a pond near the projects that we moved to. He was out on a nearby icy pond with some cousins. The ice was thin. While playing on it, Danny fell in.

Manny, the oldest of the cousins, rescued him from the hole. Manny carried him back to our apartment and knocked on the door. Mamma answered it, and took him from Manny's arms. Manny's lips were blue; his coat caked with water and ice. Manny didn't stay to explain anything to mamma. He backed out of the room as she turned Danny into a warm bath.

I treated Danny special after that. We all did. I loved all my big brothers dearly. Even when a brother ran away and left me in the center of a gang, who were converging on me, with their pit bulls growling. I loved him anyway.

I remember telling my oldest brother, Luis, that he should run for president. In MY eyes, they were all sinless. They always protected me when someone was mean to me. I stuck close to my brothers. They taught me to punch first, and ask questions later.

Mamma spoke only Spanish to us. Since we had just moved again, it made it hard to get what was required of the teachers. Mamma couldn't communicate with my new teacher, who was not fluent in Spanish.

Notes were sent home to mamma about my swearing and my daydreaming in class. Unfortunately for me, they were in Spanish and she could read them. I needed her signature before I could go back to school.

It took a bit of courage, but I got her signature, and got back in class- and back in trouble.

Mother was so exasperated by my daydreaming in school that she threatened to beat me. She would grab me by the back of the neck. She would slap the top of my head. But she never beat me.

My older brothers were also getting into trouble with their teachers. Mamma tried to take a firmer hold on us. She worked hard, and took on overtime when she could. Joseph had stopped coming home most nights now, and mamma was doling out more chores around the house for us to do. She insisted on the house being clean, regardless of how many people came in and out of it. I couldn't see why that was important. And I didn't want to do my homework.

Mamma was always asking me, "Antonio, what are you up to? You better start on your homework."

Eventually, things did change as I got close to my twelfth birthday. There was no more dancing for mamma. I took up breakdancing for a while and took wrestling in school and was undefeated and all our team

I admit, I was becoming even more rebellious as time went by. I met the wrong people and started acting up. Mamma voiced her concerns to my older brothers. "Your brother is not going to school like he says. He even told me that he wants to quit school."

Since I wasn't doing well in school, and I planned to drop out when I turned thirteen, I was no longer willing to struggle for a decent grade.

I was small, but I had huge ideas. Maybe I could get a job and help my mother more. Or, I figured that it wouldn't hurt her if I secretly sold drugs. When I told her that I could make money, she was not impressed.

"Mamma, I could help you pay the bills. I am going to be thirteen soon, and I could do errands for people. I know kids who are thirteen and work," I explained. "I could sell way more cans than I do now."

"Antonio (Rey Bendecido), it is against the law for you to stay out of school. Do you want them to take you away from me?" she replied.

I saw kids who were taken away. No, I didn't want to be taken away.

When the YMCA was open, I would go in and practice kickboxing or wrestling with other kids. When that was closed, I would hang out in the cemetery or the junkyard after school.

One day, my gang of friends found an old van that would be perfect for our clubhouse. The only problem was that there was a giant engine in the center of it, but it was fairly clean inside, and there were no broken windows. My buddies said all we had to do was pick up the motor that was in the middle of the inside.

Simple; Pick up the motor and throw it out. We struggled and struggled, but it didn't budge an inch. I told them to move back out of my way. I was going to use my kickboxing skills and KICK it out.

It was my chance to help my friends. I could help them AND show them how strong I was at the same time. I was finally going to prove myself as a man. I was shot with adrenaline like no drug could ever do to me.

I picked up my leg and swung. The motor went flying out the back where the boys had opened the double doors. It hit the ground with a loud thud.

So, we set up a headquarters in that old van, talking about how we can do anything if we stick together. It was time to celebrate, so Thomas, the gang member, told me to use my moves, because we went to see a martial arts movie, and I was practicing my kicks that day.

The devil knows who is weak and easily swayed, and he also gets a special pleasure in latching on to the ones that want to truly live a Godly life. He laughed because I was the smallest of the group and the most daring so they told me lets go in that stolen van. He laughed wickedly as I felt I needed to prove myself. My childhood was digested: swallowed up forever.

It was a couple of days later when the fat man in the junkyard spotted us there. We nicknamed him Fat Joe, because he was a little overweight.

"How in the world did you boys manage to get that motor out of this van?" Fat Joe inquired.

"We did it." Thomas spoke up. "Well, really, Tony Roam did it. He kicked it out of the van."

He was puzzled. "I can't make sense of that! That is impossible." Let me remind you we all did break dancing and we got very strong doing sports as well, so those exercises help us a lot. With the help of God the bible says. 1 Corinthians 9:26 So I run with purpose in every step. I am not just shadow boxing. 9:27 I discipline my body like an athlete, training it to do what it should.

But we all insisted that it was the truth. Then, Fat Joe told us how there were three of them, all men, big men like Fat Joe, who tried to lift it out of the van and could not do it.

Just as I trust in my ability to know

And God gave me a talent for kicking, and it saved my life more than once.

Scripture verses I read in my second year included:

Psalm 56:2 says, "Mine enemies would daily swallow me up, for they are many that fight against me, o Thou, Most High." Psalm 51:5 days, "Behold, I was shapen in iniquity; and in sin did my mother conceive me."

Deuteronomy 8:2,3 says "And you shall remember all the way in which God led you these forty years in the wilderness to humble you, and to prove to you, to know what was in your heart, and whether you keep His commandments, or no."

"And He humbled you and allowed you to hunger, and fed you with manna, which you knew not, neither did your father know: that He might make you know that man does not live by bread alone, but by every word that proceeds out of the mouth of the Lord does he live."

Ephesians 6:12 says, "For we do not wrestle against flesh and blood but against principalities, against powers, against the rulers of darkness of this world, against spiritual wickedness in high places."

Job 1:7 says, "And the Lord said unto Satan, Whence comest thou? Then Satan answered the Lord, and said, "From going to and fro in the earth, and from walking up and down in it."

Psalm 105:15 says, "Touch not mine anointed, and do my prophets no harm."

John 13:12-15 says, "So after he had washed their feet, and had taken his garments, and was set down again, he said unto them, Know ye what I have done to you?"

"Ye call me Master and Lord: and ye say well: for so am I." "If then, your Lord and Master, have washed your feet; ye also ought to wash one another's feet.

"For I have given you an example, that ye should do as I have done to you."

Psalms 28:7 The LORD is my strength; my heart trusts in him, and I Am helped: Therefore my heart greatly rejoiceth; and with my song I will praise him."

Psalms 73:26 My flesh and my heart faileth: but GOD is the strength of my heart, and my portion forever."

CHAPTER FOUR

Friends

Wicked friends lead to evil ends.

- Jonathan Malm

My life as a gang member had been filled with even more excitement. I laid in the prison bed, wishing for that kind of excitement to never again enter my life.

There was a new excitement in me. I had a revelation in my third year in prison. I was seventeen when the HOLY SPIRIT, my comforter and guide, came and minister to me.

I will never forget that day. Bible study time was announced on the loudspeaker. I figured it could be interesting to hear what they had to say. Staring at the cold cement floor in my cell or going in to see smiling, kindly faces, hum... it was an easy choice. Besides, I had just asked for God to hear my prayers, to really hear me, because I was begging Him to listen.

So, I stepped into that room, designated as the chapel, and met Rudy, Rubio, Raul and Moses. My salvation was only a step away.

I was facing time for a crime, but also now facing God's disciples! God began to speak through them.

"Do you think Christ is still on the cross?" asked Raul, one of the Bible study instructors that visited the prison each week.

He was referring to the rosary and the small cross attached to the bottom of it, as he pointed to my neck.

I didn't know what he wanted me to answer. I said, "Yes." He shook his head, "No, son, He is not there. He is in heaven preparing a place for you."

Then he proceeded to tell me all about the love of Christ, and how He died for me. And He rose again. And He is also the Holy Spirit, the mighty Word speaker, who gives you words that are inexpressible; that come from deep in your heart.

Indescribable words poured forth from my mouth. Tears ran down my cheeks. I was still a teenager, and embarrassed about the tears. I rose from my knees and thanked them for all that they had shown me.

What I found in that group was unexpected, to say the least! I only went in there because the inmates said you would get special privileges, and I didn't have anything better to do. Now I saw the reason for my presence there. The group was called "God's Bridge".

It was a bridge to a second chance. A place that welcomed me for who I was. It was a place that I would go back to. "Go on in there, man. You are always talking about God, anyways, man," said a fellow inmate. He thought he had to talk me into going the first time. He said that they were good people. He told me that it would be a good thing to have on my record, too.

But, I believe I would have gone in there anyway, without any coaching from him. God would have found a way to have gotten me in there.

God showed me the error of my ways. It now struck me as strange that I had reacted so innocently when I first got locked up. I now wanted to ask God's forgiveness for every bad thing I had ever done.

And I wanted to love people. I had the emotion of love again! It filled my whole body.

I hugged mamma so hard the next day that she thought I was going to stop her from breathing.

It didn't matter who was not in agreement with me. I inhaled everyone's love and exhaled everyone's hatred. I treated them all like they should be treated with the same patience and love God showed me.

There was an inmate named Roy in a cell next to me. Roy was as mean as he could be when it came to us Latinos. He wasn't a skinhead, but he was very racist at times I felt this guy was from the Satan cult. When he looked toward me, the world went still. He would say that I was all right, at times challenging me. If there was any of us in my group that made a motion toward him, any gesture at all, his eyes would dart around for something to hurl at us.

Once, Roy got a hold of a shank, but they found it before he could do any damage to me or anyone else.

He came up behind me and grabbed me, reaching around the front to stab me. He was aiming for my heart. I had just started carrying my small pocket Bible in my upper shirt pocket. He jammed at my chest. It must have shocked him when I swung around and knocked him down. The shank hit the ground and the CO's, Correction Officers, confiscated it.

There was daily violence, even when we were threatened with solitary confinement. Vince and other inmates who spent lots of days in the hole.

When he got out, he seemed to have lost his energy. His spirit was not only lost, but I wondered about his soul. I told the leaders in the Bible study to try to work with him, and see if they can make a change in his life, like they did for me.

I was so pleased to see him in the group the following week! The meeting barely began before he began interrupting the conversation. He talked about how he needed to get out; that his family needed him. He asked if anyone could assure him of his release date being bumped up. No one could do anything about that, they told him. He got so angry that he spit on the floor three times and walked over to the door with his arms across his chest.

I could relate to the anger. I had a lot of anger when I first came. I remember going to many counseling sessions. In one of the first sessions, I was told to explore why I had gotten locked up in the first place. That was a good question.

What had I said about my gang members? Backstabbers, double-crossers, liars! I had really felt the meaning of those words. My disparaging descriptions were about Rob and Adrien. Those were my gang brothers, considered by all to be my loyal family. What they had said about me was a lie. I was not the leader of Red Alert.

I told my new pals all about it. They listened to my story, and understood the betrayal. I could express my anger to them, but I certainly could not cry.

I told them what had happened, and told them I was innocent. I remember them laughing at me, and saying that they were innocent, too.

That made me angrier. Anger that had been gone for so long had come back. Drugs had been numbing my emotions for years.

But, then, being freshly cleaned out, I felt some emotion again. And it was a raging hot anger!

I thought that Rob and Adrien were to blame. It had been their plan, their actions that caused me to get into such trouble. Why would they point their fingers at me, saying that I was the one who had the gun? ...That I, Antonio Garcia, was the one who took the fatal shot? How could anyone blame me for anything that happened that night, when all I did was go for a ride? How could they not remember what happened?

Did you fire the gun that killed the victim? Did you think that Rob or Adrien had planned to shoot someone? Did you know the victim, that he was a corrections officer? I told the police over and over, - no, no, no, and I did not know.

My two pals and I were going to hunt someone or something down. Whether it be for a girl, drugs, a fight, or for something else, I wasn't sure. A typical night would usually hold some excitement, and I did hope for some excitement back then.

This was the true story about that night: I thought it was going to be a fun time. What usually occurred were girls and drugs, and more girls and drugs after that. I wasn't sleeping at home that often anymore, so I didn't have to ask permission to do anything. The night was clear - my head was cloudy with pot. The next thing I knew was that Rob popped a man standing on the sidewalk. It was time to call it an evening. So, I went home and went to bed ... Just like that.

It was to be the last time that I would have a dream in that bed. It was an ordinary bed to me then...but not anymore. Luis talked to me the next morning, when they handcuffed me, telling me to be cool, and not to resist arrest.

They handcuffed me behind my back as they read me my rights. They said that they had already gotten Rob and Adrien. I was filled with despair, as I lay on my cot with a letter in my hand. It was from mamma. I held that letter for hours. Mamma told me that I needed to tell my lawyer exactly what I did, with nothing left out.

I told him everything. And, everyday I try not to relive it. Street gangs do not need to physically beat someone to recruit them. Just the enticement of making some money, getting sex, or having protection can be enough. Kids who don't have a good family life will often be told that the gang is there for them. A kid will feel like they are special. They mistake attention for love.

I heard the news about more riots and killings while I was locked up. I was sure that the children of Bridgeport, New Haven Hartford and different smaller cities needed to feel the love of God. That is what will mold them into great adults.

How God could love me despite my prison life was amazing. God must enjoy a challenge, because I would let gut reactions take hold of me before I would think: WHAT WOULD JESUS DO.

Several times I cried out to God, praying "Tell me again, Lord, so that I will remain in You." I spent four hours each day, on average, reading His word.

Martin Luther had a "tower" experience. When people wanted to take his liberties away, his friends kidnapped him and placed him in a tower. There, he wrote the New Testament in German. I hoped that the experience would lead me to something great. I meditated on this often. You could say that my reasons to be the best servant I could be were born from a prison experience.

Raul told me that he could see my potential for being one of God's apostles. I could see that, too, but I knew that winning a soul from my neighborhood would be a problem.

I had more than one glimpse of unpredictable, strange behaviors of gang members.

A gang will boast that they can protect you, but gang members are more likely to be both a victim and an offender of a crime than a non-gang member.

They will turn on you in an instant. A gang member barked at me one day, "Hey, punk, you gotta disrespect our hood that way? You're gonna pick it up, man, now." He pointed to my gum wrapper. I picked it up. Litter was still everywhere.

Your gang can protect you, but they can also get you killed. The gunmen are getting younger and younger. The boys are getting bolder and bolder.

I was in the backseat of a car once, when we happened to enter the wrong neighborhood. The back window was shot out, almost killing me. The guys jumped out to see who was shooting, but, luckily for them, the shooter ran off.

They boast that they make easy money, yet 98 percent don't. Lucky was one of the many who stood on the corner selling drugs, but never made a decent living at it.

Soon, another kid, a kid called Jason, was on the street corner…the same street corner all the drug dealers took turns standing on …for the same long hours… and he, too, was always broke.

Whether you were in a gang or not, you got a nickname. Even the corner had a name. It was "Up the Way".

"Hey, Bluesman, meet me up da way," you said when you wanted to discuss something important.

"Hi, Baby, what's your name, where are you from? Meet me Up the Way." That was if you wanted a date.

"What did you get? Meet me Up the Way," was someone wanting drugs.

Gang life was a way to feel important. I recalled one kid who was told that he should get out. The gang leader told him that they didn't want him. How he fussed and cried and begged to stay! But belonging to a gang is never up to new negotiations or concessions by the leaders.

We often need to be in that very state of sinking, of hitting our own rock bottom, before we can surface. It would be so much better if we could learn from someone else's lessons! I pray that you can do that.

Let us be lifted to a glory that God wants us to experience. And, as I must tell myself every single day of my life, STAY SURFACED! Stay out of trouble.

No matter where I go, or in what situation I am in, I must stay focused. He wants me to get out of trouble, and STAY out! I could read scripture verses all day long and not realize what time of day it was. I was learning much of His Word and studying the high school curriculum. I was into knowledge for the first time in my life. The future is what I wanted to focus on, not the past.

Yet, the past couldn't be swept under the rug. Recurring thoughts of the night of the shooting haunted me. I was willing to follow them into the car. I didn't even ask where they got the car. Most of the cars were borrowed from a relative and put back the same night. Sometimes the relatives knew that they took it, sometimes they didn't.

Yes, I was a willing participant. I was an accessory to murder. Any judge or jury would have determined that. No. It is not your child that would do such a thing, but I rode off with boys that no priest would want in their church.

I wrote all those things in my journal, then I stuck my journal under my pillow. I wished that I could have forgotten many things, but being incarcerated makes one confront old times; times that could have been deadly.

After a very short time in the first prison, I was sent to a prison out of the state, so that no one would know who I was. I was spared being murdered in the prison that the crime took place in. God surely cared for me so that I would be transferred to another city.

You don't serve a light sentence when you come from the hood. It didn't work that way. Especially when it wasn't a street person that got shot. That drive-by targeted an important man - a Corrections Officer.

The gavel went down. Guilty of conspiracy to commit murder...

Scripture verses for that third year also included: Psalm 104:4 says, "Who maketh His angels spirits and His ministers flames of fire."

1 Corinthians 15:33 says, "Be not deceived: evil communications corrupt good manners."

Psalm 51: 10 days, "Create in me a clean heart, oh God, and renew a right spirit within me."

Psalm 108:13 says, "Give us help from trouble: for vain is the help of man."

Romans 3:20 says, "Therefore the deeds of the law there shall no flesh be justified in his sight; for by the law is the knowledge of sin."

Acts 17: 23 says "For I passed by, and beheld your devotions. I found an altar with this inscription, TO THE UNKNOWN GOD." 1 Timothy 2:1 says, "I exhort therefore, that, first of all, supplications, prayers, intercessions, and giving of thanks, be made for all men."

Psalms 14:1-3 says "The fool has said in his heart there is no God. They are corrupt. They have done abominable works, there is none that doeth good."

Matthew 10:31 says, "Fear not, therefore, ye are of more value than many sparrows."

Genesis 1:17 says, "And God set them in the firmament of heaven to give light upon the earth."

Mark 5:9 says, "And He asked him, What is thy name? And he answered, saying, "My name is Legion: for we are many."

CHAPTER FIVE

Mercies

I rolled over on my cot that seemed smaller every year, trying to sleep. But Holy street through street, a drug infested area of dealers who sold heroin and cocaine to children, smothered any chance of sleep. I was all-too-familiar with the activities coming from rooming houses and abandoned stores and houses. There was Sam "Diamond" Jennifer, Ramiro, (blue) James, (Bike) Timmy, (Juice), Jesica (China), and several others working the streets.

Bridgeport is where mamma is now where mamma is with me, a son that didn't listen. If I could just protect her…Oh, how I wished I was at home with mamma again! I didn't care if I would have to sleep on the floor, next to her bed.

With the veil of deception lifted from my eyes, I saw the corner for what it was. I wondered who would be left when I got out, and who would be dead or in jail.

Clifford stood on the corner every day, all day, selling drugs. He never moved. He never went to play basketball with us. He was there early in the morning. He stayed until past dark. Day after day, month after month. Until one day, he wasn't there anymore.

Some of us went to his funeral. His mother couldn't afford much, but she gave him a small service, just the same. She probably took out a loan. That is what good mothers would do.

Others let the government bury them in Potter's field. It's a public cemetery for homeless people, stillborn babies and unclaimed remains.

There were inmates coming in all the time, telling us which gangs they were in, not by words, but by their tats and their colored bandanas. Red Alert had established itself as a prison gang to protect its members, like me, from being attacked by the other gang groups inside.

At first, I was alone when I went to the visitation room. Later, I had two bodyguards escort me back and forth for my safety.

On one of mamma's monthly visits, she told me that Ice was sick with diabetes. I guess she wanted me to know about all my old friends, because she told me that Rob and Adrien's mammas weren't planning to go visit them.

I have forgiven Rob and Adriens. I understood why they said what they did. But, at the time mamma had told me this, I thought it was quite pleasing to me.

She said that Sonia, Rob's girlfriend, was pregnant. How would he handle that information? I wondered.

We talked about so many of the young girls in our community getting pregnant. Catholics and the poor don't breed high birth control users.

If there was ever a time that I could talk to my mamma, really TALK to her, it was now. My head wasn't cluttered from drugs. My loyalties were in proper order.

"Mama, I know you love me, but it was always in the back of my head that you loved Ralf and NO she loved all of us the same. Mother's just always know something different about son's and daughter's. More than me. I heard you tell someone, once, that he was your favorite."

"Oh, my love, no, I love you like the desert loves the sea. You are like fresh water to drink whenever I want to. You were a good boy. You were always right there to be my helper. It is just, well, sometimes I was not thirsty for you. I admit, there were times that you got to be too much."

I was glad we were having this talk. I was proud of her. She could speak so eloquently in Spanish.

I didn't have my dad to talk to, but mamma always did a good job consoling me. She would never abandon me. You find out who really cares for you, when you get in trouble. No one came to visit me except for my mamma and Savior's.

They had to search for mamma and Savior's each time. A guard led them to a small round table, where I was waiting for them. We talked about family. We talked about asopao, the Puerto Rican soup mamma made.

Yes, I do recall that she had said, "Antonio, honey, we all hope that this will be over soon. They will check the fingerprints on the gun, and you will be set free."

And you will be set free. I wrote in my journal: "And you will be set free. That was four years ago."

They never checked the fingerprints. The judge told me that he was going to make an example out of me. This kind of crime will not be tolerated in this city, he barked emphatically.

I can't ignore the mercies God made for me. With a new lawyer, my sentence was reduced from twenty years to twelve, with possibility of parole after six. Mamma confided to me that she had to get money from the family to hire a new lawyer, because the first one showed up at her door with white powder still sticking to his nose.

Jordan had told me to fight wicked thoughts, so I prayed, "Let my sleep come, Lord. Please, Father God, give me good thoughts."

Before I opened my eyes again, I wanted to have a **good** dream.

I tried to think of happier times. I thought back to when I passed the third grade. We planned an exciting farewell party that same week. Mamma hosted it herself, but it was for our family. People congratulated us for heading out to Connecticut. A girl kissed me on the lips. My best friend and playmate, Mark, was there, too. We had lots of fun, wrestling around with one another. Then the party was over, and we packed our things.

We moved to Hartford, when I was twelve years old, with my Godmother and mama's best friend. We went into the housing projects that were surrounded by gang activity. Mamma had said it was temporary, but it became more of a permanent situation.

Some teachers were mean to me, getting frustrated, even angry because I refused to read out loud. They saw me as dead weight in a class of more promising students. I wasn't worried about the teachers, though, as much as I was about the bullies let me remind you I was this little skinny boy who looked a lot younger 5 times let's say As David said to Goliath. (David and Goliath memories the word he expresses) 1 Samuel 17:45 'Thou come to me with a sword, and with a spear, and with a shield; but I come to thee in the name of the Lord of hosts, the GOD of the armies of Israel, whom thou has defied (Disrespected).

One day, I got bullied by a different kind of classmate. She was teasing me about my clothes being like a nerd's, and we began to scuffle with each other in the coat closet. I was on top of her when the teacher opened the door. She thought we were doing something nasty! She grabbed me by the ear and yanked me up.

I was flattered when the girl told the teacher to leave me alone, that I was her boyfriend. So, she became my girl, and I walked her home every day. (The teacher sent a note home to mamma.)

Kids always walked each other home, whenever possible. It could mean a matter of life or death. When I got a bit older, my gang walked me home. Danger was always right around the corner.

Like the day that I got into an argument with one of the dealers on the corner, and he put a 45 pistol to my temple and I picked him up stupidly and could have got killed that day. My brother's Red Alert came around the corner, causing the guy to put the gun down, and he was surrounded, so he put his gun back in his pants, and left the area or would have gotten killed and I as well. Being in gangs is no joke. It is very serious any moment you can die or be paralyzed. GOD was always here in my life…

I have another but a good memory. It was the day I got new tires for my bike. I focused on that, like my brother told me to do. I felt like a superhero on that bike! I took it out on the busy streets of Hartford because I didn't want to hit someone on the sidewalk. Truthfully, it was much more exciting to zoom the streets.

The streets of Hartford were more colorful than West Hartford. There were stores that had giant Latino faces painted on the window coverings, and the tattoo parlor had a huge multicolored sign in front of it.

Mamma fretted about me using that bike. She calmed down when she saw my brother Danny take charge of the handlebars, and put me on the crossbar to get a ride. But I had enough of that kind of riding after a couple of trips to the store, and I took off on the bike myself. Each day I got bolder, going onto busier and busier streets.

The tires were still new when a car hit the back of the bike, causing me to sail off into the air, and Ralfy ran over to me-only to get his leg stuck between the spokes.

The driver ran to my aid and asked if I was okay. I didn't have a scratch on me. He told me that he could take me home in his car, but I thanked him and said no. He went on his way as Ralfy and I tried to straighten the bent bike.

Since nothing awful had happened, and since we weren't supposed to ride on any busy streets in the first place, I didn't say anything to mamma. Mamma took the bike away from me when Ralfy told her. She said that no matter what the reason, I should never, ever, let a stranger take me into his car. What happened? She told me never to let a stranger touch me again.

The next week I was playing with the kids in the front of our unit, when a man pulled up in his car. He asked if any of us would be willing to help him get something out of his trunk, and he would buy them ice cream cones. Two little ones ran over to help him, and I went with them. The fat man with thick glasses showed us the box and told us to put it in the back seat of his nice luxury car. It wasn't even heavy. He then said that we should all hop in and go with him to get the ice cream cones he promised us. I remembered my mamma telling me to be careful about strangers. As the two small children started to get into his back seat, I grabbed both of their hands and pulled them back. Then we all ran.

Before that episode happened, a family member told me that some stranger tried to get her into his car, so I figured out that such an occurrence happened a lot in my neighborhood.

I didn't share that story with mamma, because I didn't want to upset her. I reasoned that my silence to mamma about bad things was to keep her from being upset.

She took my bike away! Ralf told her what happened. I finally got the bike back the next month, but it took promises that I never would keep.

"Mamma, my bike, mamma, please, mamma, please, please just let me fix it," I repeated. Then I swore. It was under my breath, but mamma managed to hear it.

"You are usually such a good boy. Hiding things from me is not acceptable. Go to church, Antonio, and ask for forgiveness." Dip your finger in the water, touch it to your forehead … Father, Son and Holy Ghost. The priest listens to all confessions. The priest has been anointed by God. His head was anointed with oil. My forehead, well, it wasn't anointed with anything. See the priest leaves his side of the booth? You have just been forgiven. Back then, I could not imagine a priest ever sinning. I had thought that I might grow up to be a priest.

Priests take vows of poverty. I had that down. I didn't even like to own a bunch of books, and didn't want to eat expensive ground beef because it looked like worms. And the celibacy vow did not seem unappealing to me at the time. The third one, the vow of obedience; now that would be a major step.

Priests were the best role models in my childhood. They walked the walk and talked. But being a real, positive, effective role model requires one to try to be around the person you want to integrate your beliefs upon. And priests didn't have time for me. My older brothers became my role models.

In my last years on this earth, I want to also be their role model.

In the last part of my fifth year incarcerated, I studied these scriptures, as well as many, many others.

Psalm 105:15 says, "Touch not mine anointed, and do my prophets no harm."

Leviticus 4:3 says, "If the priest that is anointed does sin according to the sin of the people; then bring for his sin, which hath sinned, a young bullock without blemish unto the Lord for a sin offering."

1 Peter 1:4 says, "As obedient children, do not be conformed to the passions of your former ignorance."

Psalms 34:17 says "If you belong to Him, God will always listen when you call Him for help."

Psalms 55:22 says, "God is glad to carry your burdens and give you the daily strength you need."

Matthew 19:26 says, "But Jesus beheld them, and said unto them, with men this is impossible; but with God all things are possible."

1 Corinthians 1:5 says, "That in everything you are enriched by Him, in all utterance, and in all knowledge."

CHAPTER SIX

Poverty

I was glad that we could stretch out in the courtyard for an hour each day. I was bursting with unspent energy. I was always full of endless energy. The gym was not always up for grabs, and my cell floor had a stickiness to it that I didn't want to get down and check out. But the courtyard had a basketball court, a track, and bars you could do chin-ups on.

It was time for lights out, and I wished I was a small child again. I wished that the voice over the intercom was my mama's voice, telling me goodnight. Then, I could cover my face with my sheet and pretend I was sleeping. As soon as mamma left the room, I would uncover my face and play with my marbles.

Diverting attention to amusement was what a child does. That is what makes him a child. But mamma told me that I was different from other kids. I was exceptionally fascinated by what others were doing, whether it be work or play. Is that what she meant? I was very interested in singing and dancing and drawing – an artsy child. Is that what she meant? Or could it have been that I was persistently gripped by demons and angels, and they seemed to be fighting for my soul?

I couldn't sleep with all the racket going on down the hallway. I watched an inmate get stomped on by guards and dragged across the floor to a private room.

One nightmarish idea followed another, until I was finally able to think about something good in my childhood. I recalled when I had a vision of an angel going up the steps to Auntie's room. I was only half awake as my thoughts became my movie theater. Recently I went to the theaters and saw a movie that had me in tears crying.

I remember writing The Best Servant Story when that angel stood by the kids, Jim Caviezel (Tim Ballard) to remind me of the voice of a loving moms who has always been my guardian angel and brothers, and my aunt's prayers. As I was incarcerated the reminder of the movie (Sound of Freedom) no hope at times, but GOD sending soldiers to pull you out with prayer and service and not expecting help from nowhere. Then the LORD who's there at times with this young man myself, Antonio, will go to different prisons and see miracles from the favor of GOD and at times, It will be like heavenly angels around my existence.

I remember how I was dreaming about Puerto Rico again. I was back in Auntie Bella's house. At the same time every night, Auntie would always say that she was going to pray for us. She would say goodnight, then climb the stairs to her bedroom.

The echo of her singing as she went up . Then, began to mix with a supernatural voice, as she was praying. I asked mamma who Auntie was getting ministered by , but she said that it was just Auntie (Tia) praying. I didn't tell mamma what I heard no one.

I thought about mamma; about the struggles she had in life. Rape is the most common crime in Puerto Rico. She didn't talk about it, but I wonder about that now. I know that she was glad to be in America. Joseph and mamma felt it was best for all of us. In America, her children would not starve.

Mamma had grabbed the hem of the single mother world more than once, only to get shoved aside. But she never stopped trying...never stopped hoping. She worked hard in factories, and was always glad to kick off her shoes when she got home.

But mamma always took time to show an interest in our lives. Never stop being involved in your child's life. If you can't give them the best, then give them *your* best.

It is twice as difficult to keep your child away from any criminal behavior when they have been raised in a nothingness. I say nothingness, because that is what poverty seems like. The kids on television have fancy toys and good cereal. Your child has nothing.

Adults in poverty struggle to be honest and loving. They double bolt their doors during the day. Legal thievery goes on in the hood. The little store lets them charge a food bill, but the prices are twice as high as the store in the better neighborhoods. When the food bill is due, at the beginning of the month, it takes away almost all of one's paycheck, leaving them with nothingness.

The most important possession I had was my bike. I got it because someone trashed it. I got my bike out of the same frozen pond that we all played on during our first winter in Hartford, the same pond that Danny had fallen into. It was stuck in the ice when I first spotted the handlebars. The ice thawed, and Danny pulled it out of the water for me.

I had been watching that bike all winter, visualizing myself riding it. We would walk on the ice, stomp on it, and walk back home. As the weather warmed, we would slide across the sheet as gently as possible. One day, the bike began to float. I tugged and tugged on it. Danny grabbed it, too, and out it came.

I had to beg my mother to let me keep the bike, because there was no place to put it, except in the already crowded bedroom. I finally had something of my own, and I planned on keeping it. I sold tin cans to save money for tires.

The lean times that many of us have faced has often been reason to abandon a Bible. But the Bible is the only true material possession that we should treasure. How faithful and strong is a servant of the Lord who can suffer through hardship and remain steadfast!

Raul had encouraged me to start a journal. He said that if I put it all on paper, I might see what I wanted to do. I wrote some Bible verses in the journal, then wrote "I don't want to be noticed. I want to survive."

I painfully realized that my whole life had taken an abrupt and permanent turn. Prison life was full of gangs, too, but I was no longer trying to fit into any group or gang. The gangs in there were pushy. Some guys had to join because of force. They kept trying to recruit me, but I resisted.

One guy took my sneakers. I demanded that he give them back, but he refused. After watching my behavior for a week, he gave me another pair of sneakers. He said that he thought I was a fighter, but that he was wrong. The sneakers he gave me belonged to another inmate, who saw me wearing them. I offered to give them back, but he told me to just keep them, because he was being released real soon.

Threats to my life happened on a regular basis, regardless of how often they moved me. I went from Moulin County Jail to Bridgeport County Jail to New Haven County Jail to Hartford County Jail, to Facility after Facility, until even my lawyer could barely keep track of me.

Inmates could see me grow in stature and strength. I would be surrounded by my Latino brothers, and they, in turn, were protected by me. The brothers who went to A.A. meetings with me were comfortable with who I was. They told their own gang to leave me be, that I wanted to be left alone.

Closing my journal, I thought about the day I first entered the first prison gates. I thought about that, and how much I had grown since that time.

I stuck out like a sore thumb in that line up. The others were twice my size. At least I was circumcised. Burly men, thickset men, muscle- bound men, all the men who had joined me in the lineup, were all respectful to me. After I was permitted to redress, one of them spoke to me.

"Hey, kid, watch out," came from the first guy. "What's up, boy, you better look out," came from the second one. These comments could have been misconstrued as threats. I, however, took them as warnings and concern for my safety. "Thanks, man," I replied, but I wasn't afraid of anyone, but very careful.

During my first introduction to time out in the courtyard, I found out their names.

It wasn't long before both Cuba and Chino became my closest friends. Chimos, child molesters, were not welcomed by any inmate group, and they considered me a child. They would sit with me when I ate. They were in the gym with me when I wanted to go in there, trying to pump up my dwarf-sized deltoids. We stuck together because that is what you do in prison. You find a few guys to watch your back.

Some inmates wanted to sell me things. When they found out that I had no way of paying for anything, they left me alone.

I had tried to keep those types of acquaintances at a distance. But what would I do about all my family members that were selling stuff? When we had a party, and mamma said we would have one, I knew I would see them again.

The odds were stacked against Cuba Te. Both of his brothers were also serving prison time. He had plans for his future and it was called revenge.

What you did to get in here, Cuba told me, is kept to yourself. No one wants to know what you did. All they had to do was ask me, and I would tell them all. I hadn't grasped his hidden meaning.

Little did I know that I was supposed to never ask inmates anything personal. I was to never try to touch their shoulder or shake their hand.

I was able to get into the gym for a little bit of time each week, and I made the most of that time. If they see my muscles, I thought, they will leave me alone. Every prison I went to had a gym. Some gyms were always crowded. Inmates as well as guards who were on their breaks were in some of them.

In lockup, you see guys practicing kicks and punches, too. I knew guys, like me, who wanted to pack on intimidating muscles in prison. Once I got home, I would work out with Ralf who was now a martial arts instructor and good street fighter.

I spent hours every week doing push-ups on the filthy floor of my cell, while my first cellmate chuckled at me. By the end of my stint, I had large biceps.

My body was healthy. It was always healthy. My mother made sure that I cared for myself from my teeth down to my private parts.

I recall, vividly, the day she and Ralfy convinced me to go in and get circumcised. I was twelve years old. That is why I have recurring thoughts on this subject.

I remembered that I went to school the very next day that I got circumcised. My mother told me that I was to stay in bed and rest. That is what the doctor told her that I should do. But I pestered her until she let me go. I couldn't bear staying in bed all day long, even if it meant going to school.

My friend and I were walking home after school one day, when an older kid came up behind us. He was picking on my friend, stepping on the back of his heels. He was calling my friend names, but my friend didn't say anything back. We kept on walking until I couldn't take it anymore.

I turned around and threw the hardest punch I could - right on his chin, and then took off running! Later on, I thought about how foolish that had been, because if he had hit me in the groin I would have been back in the hospital.

I bullied kids, too, but always had justification for my behavior. Bullying may not kill the victim, but they can destroy one's personality and self-esteem. I know that the Bible says to pray for bullies, so that you won't be burdened with hating them. It cannot be done on my own strength. I need God's wise help in that regard, always being mindful that God circumcised my heart.

This is the only wonderful circumcision in my life. For Christians, circumcision is not one thing. It is not just foreskin being removed. God goes further when He states that circumcision needs to be done on the heart.

God will usually work on our heart before He can work outward. We use the sterile, clean, knife of His word to be circumcised.

Yet, sometimes he works on the outside of us first, then goes inward. Take, for example, Saul, who, in Acts, was persecuting the Christians until God blinded Him.

We all spent 22 hours a day in our cells, playing cards or reading something. Prisons give you manuals of rules, and mine was read several times. I learned the guidelines. I was to never get in any fights, or my time could be lengthened.

But I had gotten into fights. I never bullied anyone in prison, but bullying played a part in my first fight.

It was one fight I won't forget. But not because I was thrown into solitaire. It was because I was wrong about who the bully was. My friend, Cuba, was taking blows from a skinny guy, when I jumped in and started punching. The unwritten code is that you always defend your friends from bullies. The skinny guy was being bullied by Cuba, though, I found out later.

Another fight I was in was when some guy took my phone time. Each inmate has a very limited amount of phone time assigned to him, and the dude would get on the phone during my time. I flipped out the third time it happened, tying the phone cord around his neck.

At one time in my life, I tried to learn a new way to relate to bullies. I remember when I was back in McDonough Elementary School, wanting, so desperately, to make friends.

I sat in my class, daydreaming, and trying to find excuses to talk to any kid around me. That included the bullies. They never had anything nice to say to me, but I didn't care anymore.

I thought that I needed to include them in my life, so, when mama put on one of her many parties, I invited a few of them to my house.

You had to watch them closely, as mamma reminded me to, to make sure they weren't going to steal anything. One kid told my brothers and me that he owned my bike. "That bike is mine. I recognize it. It is the same bike I stole from T-bone awhile back."

It was good that he was outnumbered, because he didn't press the issue. We had worked too hard for that bike, and it wasn't going to go anywhere. I loved that bike, flat tires and all.

I read many scriptures about God's knowledge and wisdom, and on circumcision, the end of the fifth year of lock up. Some of those scriptures included:

Proverbs 4:23 says, "Keep thy heart with all diligence: for out of it are the issues of life.

Ezekiel 36:26 says, "A new heart shall I also give you, and a new spirit will I put in you: and I will take away the stony heart out of your flesh, and I will give you a heart of flesh."

Deuteronomy 10:16 says, "Circumcise therefore the foreskin of your heart, and be no more stiff-necked."

Romans 2:25 -29 says, "For circumcision verily profiteth, if thou keep the law; but if thou be a breaker of the law, thy circumcision is made uncircumcision. Therefore, if the circumcision keeps the righteousness of the law, shall not his uncircumcision be counted for circumcision?

"And shall not uncircumcision which is by nature, if it fulfills the law, judge thee, who by the letter and the circumcision dost transgress the law? For he is not a Jew, which is one outwardly; neither is that circumcision, which is outward in the flesh; But He is a Jew, which is one inwardly and circumcision is that of the heart, in the spirit, and not in the letter, whose praise is not of men but of God."

Psalm 147:5 says, "Great is our Lord, and of great power: His understanding is infinite."

Job 37:16 says, "Do thou know the balancing of the clouds, the wondrous works of Him which is perfect in knowledge?" Joshua 5:2 says, "At that time the Lord said to Joshua, "Make flint knives and circumcise the Israelite men again." The breakdance instructor had been asking about me. You might think that breakdancing wasn't a positive thing in my life, but it was. Breakdancing was good, clean fun. I surely needed that, back when I was only about eleven years old. Ralf and I were at the YWCA, horsing around, when we saw some boys that were breakdancing. These were boys who took the art seriously enough to practice fervently, every day. Ralf and I caught on quickly, and we joined them the next day. There were a few adults at the Y that enjoyed watching us. One man, named,

Ramon was the one who would holler out, "Good job, boys, great, you are doing so great!"

We needed a coach to make us better, so Ramon stepped in to become our manager. He saw our potential. Because of all the practice, Roger said we had the skills to enter contests. I was thrilled to be a part of something so vibrant. The administrator of the Y paid us to be mentors to small boys, like a big brother in the Big Brothers association. I was always on my best behavior when I did things with the smaller boys. It was probably mentoring me as much as it was them.

Mamma started to take an interest in it. It made her happy to see Roger come to the door to get me. Though she spoke very broken English, and Roger was not affluent in Spanish, they were able to communicate. She sensed that she could trust him to take her two youngest boys.

Breakdancing began in the 1970's in the Bronx by primarily the Puerto Ricans. Many of them were former street gangs, such as Black Spades, the Young Spades, and Baby Spades. This was my other gang, my breakdancing gang: Wiz Kid, Pop, Crip, Papo, Moe D, Richie Rich, Tic A Lot, Smurf, Ralf and me (Tony Roam) - 10 of us. And Roger was going to take us to the top. pushed us to practice, and we gave ourselves the name DYNAMIC BREAKERS. That summer, we shined.

We entered a contest at the YMCA and won enough money for Ramon to buy us bright breakdancing costumes. We went on the road. Ramon took us to Massachusetts. We even got on three television shows. One of them you have probably heard of: The Jerry Lewis Telethon.

When we all had nothing going on for any upcoming shows, guys began to get involved with other things, girls, and street life and stopped coming to practice. That's when trouble came our way and a lot of things didn't go right to where we all fell away one by one from the group of Dynamic Breakers and some even became part of the gangs.

CHAPTER SEVEN

Faith

I was counting the days down. I put in my journal, "I have five more days before mamma is going to pick me up, and the visit she made today will be her last one."

We talked about the things I was going to keep busy with, such as the job my brother lined up for me.

We kept the conversation positive, and mamma told me that Roger took us up to Canada on his own dime. Roger and his girlfriend drove us over long stretches of highway and into campsite after campsite, where we sometimes got to go out on boats.

The campsites all had a spot where Roger could make a nice fire. He would have us sit around and he would start to talk about personal things; moral things. One question he would ask us often was what kind of person we wanted to become. He would talk about us making right choices in our lives.

As the summer was close to an end, a couple of the guys dropped out. Roger tried to prevent this from happening by having a talk with their parents, but it didn't help. There were other boys who wanted to join our group, to take their place, but none of us agreed to it. Roger went along with our decisions.

I had an idea who I wanted and who I didn't. The boys that left were talented and smart. I wanted replacements to be as good as they were. Papo was the best of the group, and I wanted him back. But, even when the boys and I went to Papo and pleaded with him to come back, he refused.

As we got better, and older, the girls that dropped in to see us dance began to ruin our concentration. Tony Roam me especially loved the girls. Roger called me a *ladies' * man. Moe D would often cut his practice short so that he could go hang with a girl.

I would have run off when Roger did, but I didn't want to make Roger upset. He told us that girls would always be there, but the opportunities would not.

Roger wasn't just our manager; he was a good man to all of us. We all thought so highly of him that we did him an honor. We gave him a nickname. We called him Pepsi because he drank a lot to this day, we all respected him greatly.

He was always telling me to be careful. "Be careful, Tee watch your back when you walk home alone," Or "Be careful, son, you don't want to get into trouble with the cops." So, when Papo dropped out, then Richie Rich, Roger was unhappy. and, when Rock went into his home and stole things, Roger wondered if he should give it up, too.

Soon, no one was left for him to manage but Crip, Ralf and myself. We watched the whole thing fall apart, and couldn't do anything to stop it. Roger moved away, so I never saw Roger again for a long time. I was sure that I would always have a special place in my heart for him. I will always remember the man who introduced me to the Arts of music, and taught me how to breakdance to it.

He gave me some stage advice and street advice, but his words of warning didn't really resonate in my mind; Not until it was too late. The opportunities to get in trouble far outweighed the positive things. I know now that being good at something, whether it be breakdancing or walking in Christ, takes much practice.

I ate my lunch on a plastic plate with a plastic spoon, though much of the time all I could smell was the toilet, thinking about Roger. He was like a father to me.

Pretty soon, I thought as I looked around, and I won't have to be in this small cell anymore. I looked at the size of it, which was the size of an average bathroom. Two long strides will get you across it.

I had grown quite tall, and was anxious to play a good game of basketball with my friends and David.

I was sick of playing against inmates who were out to demoralize me. Some were overpowering bullies, some weren't quite as much. But it would soon be time for me to leave this macho culture and get back to the gym at the Y. It was my last week to have male bodies so close to me that I could smell their sweat. I spent every noon hour in a yard full of tough guys.

I wasn't implying that I felt threatened in the yard. I never had to feel endangered, because we were well guarded. The Latino gangs were on one side, and the black gangs were to themselves on the other. The whites, who didn't reside in Cheshire much, were outnumbered, and stood closer to the guards.

I was also taught in the Bible study that God was watching over me. He would step in for me in times of trouble. And, if something should go wrong, I guess God was going to take care of me in heaven, too.

I had learned that if you never lived for Christ, but you get saved later in life, you will go home to be with the Lord. If you are saved at twenty or at age sixty, well, it doesn't matter.

For it is not by works that we are saved, but by faith. The first will be as valued as the last...

Some of the inmates I met really deserved punishment, but most of them could have been led to repentance and faith in Jesus. I watched some of the toughest guys break down and accept Christ.

It was a miracle that some of those men were saved at all. Young men who are gang members suffer unprecedented rates of mental illnesses. The lack of education and proper health care is also staggering.

I knew young men on the outside that wanted to change their lives around. I could understand that feeling. I felt a bit guilty about not wanting to change for so long, too.

When I felt guilty about my bad behaviors, I desired to confess, apologize, and try to make amends to those I wronged. I was able to see the wrongs others were making as things that were also fixable.

I laid on my cot, thinking about all this. Jesus was an example for me. He had been pointing things out for me to concern myself with. You could say He placed a burden on my heart. I knew that the Bridgeport, New Haven and Hartford Connecticut locations were where I needed to minister. The streets were my calling. Southern New York was bad, but downtown Bridgeport, Ct. was worse.

Raul had said, "Whether you are discouraged and brokenhearted, being unjustly thrown into a life of poverty or a life of crime, there is hope. The Word tells us that all things are possible for those who love God."

With that in mind – having the scripture instilled in me, and knowing the undying love that Jesus gives me, I was determined to conquer any overwhelming difficulties in life.

But, what about my family? I had grown to love all my family, as you do with your own.

I wasn't a little child. Children are resilient. I remember the days that I could easily spring back. I could be inconsolable one minute over a terrible event, and go happily on my way to the next. It was going to be very difficult to bounce back from this.

What would I do about my gang friends? How could I get them to believe that I wanted no more of gang life, but that I still cared deeply for each of them?

What will people treat me like? People aren't going to care about what I say if I don't act like I am saved. That is why some say the church is full of hypocrites. People who talk the talk but do not walk the walk give the church a bad reputation.

There are people in churches with gang mentalities. They sit on their own side, with their own group of friends. The people on the other side are not in agreement with them on how certain things in the church should be done. That is not the kind of church I planned to find. I wanted to find a church that would love me as much as I loved them.

I was afraid of what the church would think of my ignorance in the Word. I figured that if I would move at a steady pace toward God, my life would be moved to a better place. I was preparing to be a great servant, physically and spiritually, as I could feel that I was growing daily in my knowledge of His word.

Maybe, I would sit silently in a pew when I went to church. Maybe, I wouldn't speak until spoken to.

"Heart is just a beeping heart, but a spiritual heart makes a big difference"

- Pastor Antonio Garcia

Here are some of my scripture verses in the last year of lock up:

1 Corinthians 15:33-34 says, "Do not be deceived: Evil company corrupts good habits."

"Awake to righteousness, and do not sin; for some do not have the knowledge of God. I say this to your shame." Hebrews 10:24 says, "And let us consider one another to provoke unto love and to good works."

Proverbs 25:11 says, "A word fitly spoken is like apples of gold in pictures of silver."

Romans 14:12 says, "So then every one of us shall give account of himself to God."

2 Corinthians 9:8 says, "And God is able to make all grace abound toward you; that ye, always having all sufficiency in all things, may abound to every good work."

Matthew 25:29 says, "For unto everyone that hath shall be given, and he shall have abundance: but from him that hath not shall be taken away even that which he hath."

Hebrews 2:3 says, "How shall we escape, if we neglect so great a salvation: which first began to be spoken by the Lord, and was confirmed unto us by them that heard Him."

Genesis 1:29 says, "And God said, Behold, I have given you every herb bearing seed, which is upon the face of all the earth, and every tree, in which is the fruit of a tree yielding seed; to you it shall be for meat."

Titus 2:11-12 says. "For the grace of God that bringeth salvation hath appeared to all men."

"Teaching us that, denying ungodliness and worldly lusts, we should live soberly, righteously, and godly, in this present world."

Hebrews 4:15-16 says, "For we do not have a High Priest who cannot be touched with feeling of our infirmities; but was in all points tempted like as we are, yet is without sin."

CHAPTER EIGHT

A Parent's Love

As I lay my head down, I try to focus on mamma. My thoughts of her love were getting me through the days. Four more days and I would be back home!

My mother wasn't old, but she treated me like Joseph was treated by his father. My brothers didn't get as much attention as I did. I sensed that mamma was always trying to protect me. I felt her protection and love, like I had guardian angels around me.

She was a good Catholic woman, and she went to mass as often as she could. She didn't force us boys to go to church. She said that she wanted us to make our own choice as to what religion we wanted to follow. But she did tell us that it would be wonderful if we went to any church.

In Puerto Rico, before we came back to America, a Pentecostal church member asked mamma if they could take us to church. Mamma agreed. Ralf and I were surprised when the people filed around us and began praying for us.

Then, the same lady who brought us there laid her hands on both of us. She was getting Ralf real nervousness, because he never heard a person speak in tongues. And, she scared him with her firm grip on his shoulder. He ran from her. I stood there, taking it all in. This demonstration of unshakable, determined prayer did not scare me.

I could tell that they were all sincere when they said that they loved me. But, I did not love them back yet.

When we got back to America, I stayed around mamma a lot. I was a young boy, and in love – with mamma. I loved her so much! If it is true that we teach people ways to treat us, I must have been teaching my mamma well. The more I showed mamma how much I loved her, the more love she poured back. I remember when I could still sit on her lap without hurting her, and sit on her I did!

She would be the first to tell you that she wasn't the best mother in the world. But she was the best mother to ME. She didn't give me her best all the time, and it was never enough for her. She had a limited amount of time on her hands, working to support us. She knew she couldn't always be there for me, so she told my brothers to be good to me when she wasn't home. For the most part, they obeyed that request.

My mamma treated me like a baby because I was the youngest, but my brothers tried to make me a tough fighter. My brothers and I were a handful of energy. She would scream at us if we wrestled under her feet, then send us out to play until it got dark.

As often as I could, I would ask mamma about my dad. "Can you please tell me about papa?" I would implore. She would always say something nice about him. Oh, he was a great cook. He was a great repairman. He was a great husband. He was a great father. He was very handsome.

She never mentioned that he was dead - *ever again*. Not after my meltdown at age four. She would hold me and tell me nothing but good things in our lives.

She would cradle me in her arms when I had bad dreams, but moms never knew that I had Epilepsy attacks, so when I became a grown man, my x wife later on found out about me. In the bathroom almost dead six months after we got married in 2012 and everyone knew and figured out why at times I would seek support for comfort and His Holy Spirit and angels were always my comforter at all times. I have had dreams of angels, of God and of vision. Through the days and still counting, I read these scriptures that supported me

Gen. 28:12 says "And he dreamed, and behold a ladder set up on the earth, and the top of it reached to heaven; and behold the angels of God ascending and ending on it."

Acts 2:27 says, "Because thou wilt not leave my soul in hell, neither wilt thou suffer thine Holy One to see corruption." Jesus Christ has been sending His spirit to many of us. You may have already sensed this.

Romans 15:14 says, "And I myself am also persuaded of you, my brethren, that ye also are full of goodness, filled with all knowledge, able also to admonish one another."

CHAPTER NINE

Why

It was the first evening that I was out, and I had already forgotten what trouble some of my friends had tried to get me into. I walked over to Rob and Adrien, who were on the corner. I could relate to my friends, so I avoided any urge to scold them.

I did think about the days when I was smoking pot with them. Though I wasn't willing to do that anymore, I dismissed their behavior as normal street life. We laughed and acted like we spent the last six years away on some island.

I didn't want to think about how my friends got in the way of helping my mother, and in the way of helping myself, too. I started at the age of thirteen, smoking pot, getting occasional drugs from friends who allowed me to take a hit or two. Then, when I was fourteen, it was more frequent. I had thought it wasn't bad, since many around me were smoking a blunt five to ten times a day. By the time I was an official gang member, I had sampled pretty much 2 different drugs on the streets.

Since my brothers already knew that I smoked and drank, I didn't have to hide it from anyone I thought. Ralf as soon as he found out I was drinking and smoking pot almost as much as I was trying cocaine with High school friends. In the lunchroom in school he scolded me and asked what I thought. My eyes got watery from the love my brother showed me that day. In front of all the classmates and schoolmates.

When I was fourteen, I had a couple girlfriends from summer break dancing practice that still followed me around. They went to school with me during the day, and went to my area after. So, I always had people selling drugs around me. Then we started being part of it not expecting it because of the needs. Since Ralf rebuked me more I started focusing then using the drugs for myself at all and learning how to fight and being tough guy.

God has forgiven me for that. He has done a lot of work on me, molding me to use us as His servant. I believe He made the cast for me when I was born, and I hadn't squeezed into it yet.

The gang all had a similar life of poverty at times and some came from good families who wanted to be part of it because of the fame street people have as you see today. Some were fatherless like myself, whose mother at times cared and some had moms who were careless for them. Some dads who use and sell drugs parents who overdose and some had caring parents who were professionals even Pastors. Rob was born to a fifteen a year-old girl that dressed him in gang colors from infancy, he never knew who his father was. I remember a cop name Ralfy, a friend who grew up in a good home, who got lock up with us one time, since that time he never went back to the ghetto and became a police officer, and some who grew up in the suburbs, but wanted to be part of it because of the fame

Piloto was on the corner, too, and welcomed me back. I remembered Piloto, who loved the girls, but hated the fighting, asking me to go to a sweet sixteen party with him at the Catholic church just off Kenny street. These parties were a major deal, and people dressed up like they were going to a formal ball.

Piloto was almost sixteen when he was invited to that girl's party from our school. She invited her whole class, too. Though I was younger than him, he couldn't find another friend who would be willing to go to a party where there were other groups.

We got our suit jackets and bow ties on, and went down into the church basement. Piloto went straight over to Lilie, a black girl in a red dress that must have cost hundreds of dollars. As they were talking, a boy came up to them, asking what the deal was.

An argument broke out. Lilie stepped in the middle of them. She had forgotten to tell Piloto that she already had a boyfriend. I grabbed Piloto by the arm and told him we had to get out of there. But the door was blocked by several other groups of boys coming toward us. I could see that it was a gang. The crowd backed away to let them at us. None of our gang was there. There was one boy, a kid from our area, named Creo, who knew me. When he saw us run into the bathroom, and witnessed the gang trying to break the bathroom door down, he ran and got help. He ran to a friend's house that was a member of the biggest gang in town. It happened to be one of the biggest gangs not to be mentioned.

The gang came with knives, shovels, and guns, coming up to the church door. One of the adult chaperones had called the police, and we could hear sirens in the distance. Arguing escalated outside the door between both gangs and the chaperones.

No one knew if the chaperones would also get hurt. It seemed like neither side wanted to hurt them, but it could easily be done if they kept standing in the middle.

The police came before that happened. The gang surrounded the church as we all went outside. The police were ready to start cuffing people, but the youth leader begged them to just let us all go home. It was a church function, after all. I stood there stiffly and silently. Roger taught us boys that we were to show nothing but cooperation to a police officer. They left without arresting anyone.

It wasn't unusual for police to show up hours after a rumble started, though. There could be no one around one moment, and the next a hundred people outside. One Sunday night, a riot took place about 9 p.m. but the police didn't show up until midnight.

Because of my friends in Red Alert, I joined gang life in all seriousness. Red Alert had a tattoo of a different source put on my chest. One of the home boys did all our tats. They would break into the Tattoo parlor through the walls, doors, and ceiling to get the stuff needed. The tattoo parlor was broken into 38 times in one year. It was very hard to get good tattoo artists to work there!

I was the average age for joining a gang. New members were typically just under 15 years old. I hadn't noticed at the time, but no one joined in my hood after the age of nineteen.

The different gangs joined our gang, making it one of the largest in the states.

They had a "committee" that was the backbone of the gang. We had a President and a Vice President, and even a Godfather. I felt very cool walking with Red Alert. For the most part, people would look at us and cross the street. Gangs wore different colors. We wore special colors.

"Hi, boys. What's up?" Ice dad would say. He never avoided us.

Mamma let me go over to get kickboxing lessons with my brothers, Danny and Ralf. One thing I had to do, to get to go with them, was to get right back to school.

When I was with my gang, though, I continued to do drugs and run the streets.

I would also go on the van to a nondenominational church with Ralf and two neighbor boys his age. We picked up other children along the way, and the tiny bus got loud. We had lots of fun there, because we could cut up and clown around, and nobody said to stop it. When I got back home, I would repeat what I was told by the Sunday school teacher for that Sunday's lesson, and my brothers and friends started calling me "preacher".

That might have been a good nickname for me after I got into my late twenties. But it wasn't at that time.

Each nickname given you by the gang was well chosen. It suited your personality, your profession, your hobbies, or what you looked like. Sometimes it was just what you are a lot of.

I had my gang name. I was called Tony Roam, the uy who never had a permanent home. Your nickname was tattooed on you, as well.

If you wanted to move away from the gangs, you had to move out to the suburbs. We kept moving in the same community. Hartford was ninety percent black and Puerto Rican. People would send their buses and vans to us and take us back out to their neighborhoods and churches. I remember the church van that came to get us and me for a while.

It became apparent that something was wrong the day mamma told me to get away from the screen door.

"You and Ralf aren't going to church anymore," mamma said. "So, stop watching for that van, because it isn't coming."

I couldn't tell her what happened, so I figured if I went over to Sonia's house, she might know. Sonia was a Puerto Rican girl that was dating Cuba, and she put her little cousin on the church van when we went, but she never wanted to go.

Maybe she could shed some light on the situation. I knocked, and Sonia came to the door. She was as skinny as me, and at thirteen years old, had barely begun a woman's body. I asked her what was up with the church not wanting to pick us up anymore.

"Oh, it isn't that they don't want to, Tony, come on in and I will tell you what happened." I followed her into the front room.

I sat next to her on the couch, and she began to explain. Her ten- year- old cousin, who was picked up first but was always dropped off last, was molested by the driver. He coaxed her onto his lap after church one day, and as he spoke to her about how beautiful she was, and as he continued to whisper to her, she could feel something getting hard that she was sitting on. He stroked her and fondled her and tried to sooth her. And then he told her that she better never tell anyone about how BEAUTIFUL he found her to be, and how she made him crazy, so it was her fault. Or, he said, he would hurt her and her family.

Sonia talked slowly and deliberately. She had turned her gaze away from me. Looking out the window, she made a deep sigh. I followed her cue and turned my head away from her, looking down at her dog next to me. As I began to massage the dog's neck, I realized how silly that would have looked, and how much laughter it would have brought from my new gang, because the dog was just a stuffed toy. We weren't allowed pets in the projects.

I wondered how a man could be so evil. I wondered why people choose evil when they clearly have a choice. I thought about telling someone else, but Sonia told me that the man had been arrested already.

I never told anyone, but Sonia might have told someone.

Maybe she told Cuba. I wasn't about to ask him about that now. Piloto and I were reminiscing with Cuba and others. I urged Jose to take me over to Sonia's house to see her baby, and he said he would…right after the rap fight.

The crowd of people had been gathering for a few minutes, circling around two young men. Each was to take his turn duking it out- with a rap. Pointing his finger toward the other, the first one rapped stuff about the hood and death, and then the other one stepped in the middle of all the people, and took his turn doing his rap, trying to get the crowd to favor his skills. There would be a friendly back off when one of them was the final winner, but it might take ten or fifteen turns from each one before that was determined.

I don't know why, but I loved watching it.

Some Bible verses I looked up after my first month of release:

Matthew 25:46 says, "Then they will go away to eternal punishment, but the righteous to eternal life."

Isaiah 40:28-31 says, "Have you not known? Have you not heard? The Lord is the everlasting God, the Creator of the ends of the earth. He does not faint or grow weary: His understanding is unsearchable. He gives power to the faint, and to him who has no might he increases strength."

Psalm 10:14 says, "Thou hast seen it; for thou beholds mischief and spite, to require it with thy hand; the poor committeth himself unto thee; thou art the helper of the fatherless."

Proverbs 15:25 says, "The Lord will tear down the house of the proud, But He will establish the boundary of the widow."

Psalms 91:2-3 says, "I will say of the Lord, He is my refuge and my fortress: my God: in Him shall I trust."

"Surely, He shall deliver thee from the snare of the fowler, and from the noisome pestilence."

Psalms 22:9-10 says, "But thou art He that took me out of the womb. Thou didst make me hope when I was upon my mother's breast."

"I was cast upon thee from the womb; thou art my God from my mother's belly."

Isaiah 64:8 says, "o Lord, thou art our Father; we are the clay, and thou our potter; and we all are the work of thy hand."

Proverbs 14:19 says, "The evil will bow before the good: and the wicked at the gates of the righteous."

2 Corinthians 5:10 says, "For we all appear before the judgment seat of Christ, that each one of us may receive what is due him for the things done while in the body, whether good or bad."

CHAPTER TEN

Muscle

My gang came to our door several times in one morning. Mamma always looks through a crack in the blinds. If she thinks it is trouble, she whispers, "SHHHH," which is our alarm system. I told her not to answer the door for them today. I was getting ready for my welcome home party, and my family would be arriving soon.

I remember when my gang didn't want to hang out at my house. When they did come in for a few minutes, mamma was always staring and glaring. Now I understand her concern.

When you are a tough gangster, though, a parent's love can be a heavy weight to carry.

She was glad to not answer the door just yet, and came over to me. Mamma told me that it was good that I had quit swearing, as she touched my hand.

I hadn't been thinking about the pain it caused my mother to have to correct my cuss words. She must have cried herself to sleep some nights because of me. And I am sure that when she saw how the gang dressed and talked it gave her a feeling of revulsion. None of those things had crossed my mind before.

Back then, I was only thinking of the burden she was placing on me. It was her fault, we all reasoned, that we spent too much time in the junkyard, the streets, or the cemetery. If only she would be more welcoming! Nice, clean meeting places were hard to come by.

At ages fourteen and fifteen, Ralf and I were no longer children. Though my mother could still see trouble ahead of me, I could no longer see it. I now accepted the trash talk, the fights, the crimes, as just a part of life. I had grown to make excuses for my bad behavior, and my friend's bad behaviors. Mamma still saw me as her baby, and I hated it. That was her problem. She didn't understand street life.

Ralf always told me to never try cocaine or crack, ever again. He would have been furious with me if he had known what I planned to do. When he did find out, he did what any loving brother would do. He rebuked me that day in front of all the students that's true brother love always alert in the streets and life to one another

I remember when I wanted to go with a girl after school to try it. We hopped the bus over to her house. She lived in the West End. People on the west side had nice things. The houses were nicer. The children's clothes were nicer.

"Joy, who is your friend?" her mother asked, smiling at me. Joy told her my name and elbowed me to put out my hand to her momma.

After a bit of casual pleasantries, Joy and I went upstairs to her room. It was a beautiful room, with pillow shams and a comforter that matched. We sat down on the bed, and I stared at it while she prepared the cocaine. I dangled my legs over the side and laid my upper torso down on the bed.

"What about your mother? Isn't she right downstairs?" I asked.

"Oh, she won't find out. She is in denial. She doesn't check on me. She doesn't even know that I been working. She trusts me. If you told her I do drugs, she won't believe you," she replied. Joy, died later on from a over dose when she got older and that's the last new I heard about her.

Do you recall times that your parents had a suspicion that you were not supposed to be around certain people, and you did not see it? I was soon to experience what she had foreseen.

I was sixteen when I got arrested, and seventeen when they transferred me as a prison inmate. At the age of twenty, I had my second to the last meeting with the parole board. The Board had been informed of my religious activities, my A.A. attendance, and my N.A. attendance and I got involved with more positive program's.

There were people who thought that the timing was too convenient; that I was only acting saved because I wanted to be paroled. That was not the truth.

When I finally understood what the sinner's prayer was all about, I wanted to shout it from the mountaintops. I shared it with my fellow inmates, my family, and the correction officers. That was my step one: admit that I am a sinner, my life was unmanageable, and that I needed Jesus to die on the cross for my sins.

Many things changed after that time. An integral part of my maturity was simply facing what I had done, and that I wasn't going to be released until the age of twenty-one.

God was sensitive to what I was going through. God sent His Son to this corrupt world to save people just like me. He gave me encouragement.

God's favor upon my soul saved me from addictions and hatred. You cannot be a servant of the Lord and be on drugs or have enemies. Some plants might be good for eating, but marijuana is not one of them.

The Lord can help Christians heal from this affliction and hatred life. God watches as we take steps in the right direction. God watches where your feet are planted.

If a servant of God takes unnecessary steps, he is no longer doing that which the Lord commands him to do. He becomes self-serving.

The obstacles of drugs and alcohol put in my family's path just added to all the other obstacles that were already there, such as the joblessness that was rampant in our district. Hearts were broken because of drugs as often as the store windows were. Drugs caused depression rather than the opposite that one was seeking. When you are on drugs, you think that your life was a mistake.

Drugs have ruined the lives of people in my family. I have seen my own brothers in drug-induced stupors. I, myself, have been in drug induced stupors. Some of my family still does drugs. They say that Park street breeds addicts.

There are people who say that the war on drugs is unwinnable. It is like a plague that will never stop. But I say that we all can win the war on drugs in our own lives. It could be illegal drugs or prescription drugs that have taken hold of you. If you abuse drugs of any kind, you are being deceived by Satan. He steals our joy by convincing us that this is a fix for any ailment.

I did not possess the ability to witness others when I was first released. That first year of freedom I had to work on damage control. I had created a situation that needed tending to.

The problem was that I had been on furlough just before I was released, at the age of twenty. It was a trial furlough to see if I could handle the outside world. It was a twelve-hour furlough, and I had gotten a girl pregnant.

Some scripture verses I looked up on the morning I was release.

CHAPTER ELEVEN

The Ride Home

When mamma and Ralfy came to get me, I mentioned some things that happened to me in prison.

"Tony, you don't need to relive the past," mamma commented. I am not reliving the past, as much as I am purging it away from my existence, for the more it is shared, the less power it has over me. That is what I wanted to say.

But I simply replied, "Yes, mamma, you are right."

Believe me, God knows who you are more than you or others know who you are. Maybe someone needs to know that they are not a nobody. They might be a wretch, but not a nobody.

Maybe my writing will never amount to anything. If God and I alone see the worthiness in this book, it is well with me. God is whom I shall please.

Many people outwardly appear to want to please God, but, then, they are different behind closed doors. Do you try to please God, or others?

You can speak with spiritual eloquence, pray in public, and maintain a holy appearance…but it is your behavior that will reveal your true character.- Steve Maraboli

Do you know what salvation is? The Merriam Webster dictionary cannot begin to steer you in the right direction. It is more than just a word. It is the center core of what this world is all about - the redemption of man from the bondage of sin.

Ralf was a nonconformist, a rule-breaker, someone who took care of his health and physical well-being. That was helpful. It kept him out of trouble and away from drugs. Luis was in the Marine Corps., so he was in an accepted type of gang. Danny, lived a different life always and loved animals. Antonio, myself ready for a different journey, and coming to face Epilepsy attacks and so much more to reach where I am at.

I thought that family was either of two things: What you were born into or being a gang member. Loyalty was emphasized. And, to my surprise, I thought that after I got out of prison, my problems would be gone.

Part of this true story is that I had not been prepared for what was ahead. Oh, sure, it all started with good intentions, high hopes, and family welcomes.

That afternoon, Mamma gave me a big welcome home party. There were dozens of family members that showed up. Ice was there, too. Though Victor was there, he didn't live with mamma anymore. Mamma had a new boyfriend. He came with her on all of her visits to see me, but I really didn't know him, Yet to well.

Everyone was still eating, when I cleaned my plate with the last bite of Puerto Rican rice. The food was delicious, and I ate a full plate in about two minutes. That was how fast I was used to eating.

I wanted to tell them about the Bible that was in my hand when I first came through the door... The Bible I placed on the coffee table, but never looked at it. I wanted to witness family members, like my stepfather, Victor. I had every intention to do so.

Victor, wasn't my stepfather by marriage. Mamma would have liked it if he had married her, and we children sure wouldn't have minded. He was a jovial man, who loved life, nature and animals. He gave me dogs and pigs and other animals in Puerto Rico, and showed me how to care for them.

When he and mamma split up, it was hard on me. After I got saved, I didn't want to lose him to Satan.

I decided that I didn't want to tell him that I was saved… I wanted to SHOW him.

Victor, shared with me some of the things I had missed out on, because of the time I spent in prison. But I was already aware of things I had missed out on, and I told him that I was going to do my best not to ever miss out on anything again.

"Don't get back into that gang life, Antonio," he warned.

"No, sir," I answered, respectfully. He always said that you get what you give. I never knew what that meant until I became a man.

"Did you get your schooling done there, Ken?" he asked.

"No, sir. I tried, but I failed the GED course. I plan to try again, though."

"You get what you give, Tony," he told me, patting my shoulder.

Why did he have to go and pat my shoulder?

"So, that girl over there, what is her name, Joy? Is she pregnant with your child?" he asked. I shrugged my shoulders, as if to say, I don't know what you are talking about. "Better get a move on with a job, Joy."

He left, and, for some reason, I was glad. I knew what he meant. He didn't need to tell me. It meant that I had to make big changes in my life. And I thought I had already done that.

I waited for Shine and Ice to finish their cakes, then said good-bye to the guests that remained, and walked out the door.

Scripture verses I looked up the first month I was released: Proverb 18:14 One who has unreliable friends soon comes to ruin, but there is a friend who sticks closer than a brother.

Proverb 17:17 A friend loves at all times, and a brother is born for a time of adversity

John 15: 12-13 My command is this: Love each other as I have love you. Greater love has no one than this: to lay down one's for one's friends,"

Job 16: 20-21 " My intercessor is my friend as my eyes pour out tears to GOD; on behalf of a man he pleads with GOD as one pleads for a friend……

CHAPTER TWELVE

The Way They Make You Feel

Ralf and I left the party, meandering the streets. People would come up to me with smiles and handshakes. Girls kept wanting to touch my muscular arms. I wished, now, that people wouldn't comment about my muscles.

I left Shine and Ice at their house and went to Joy place. She was the girl who was going to have my baby. She had written to me as soon as she found out, so I had only known for a week.

I believed her. Then I doubted. Then I believed. She was four months pregnant and it showed a little. I thanked her for coming to my party, and told her I was sorry that I couldn't spend more time with her.

After visiting her, I went to the clothing store to buy her a proper dress. I asked the woman where the dresses were for pregnant girls.

"You mean maternity dresses," she snapped, pointing to a rack.

I couldn't figure out what size to get. Joy was eighteen, but she didn't look large enough for the size eighteen. Maybe, I had thought, I should get her a sixteen, since she is small. Those still looked too big. I couldn't bring myself to ask the saleslady for help, so I left without a dress.

I went to see more guys that were asking about me. No gang members ever go visit their gang members in prison, but they were busting down my door that morning.

If you are a gang member, you don't want any attention to be drawn towards you. You stay away until they are free. Then, you will ask for them.

The next day, I was invited to go along to a meeting with Red Alert. A group of us went in and sat down. After the leader spoke a while, then sat down, I stood up and said that I had something important to say. I told them that gang life, the killing and fighting, was wrong. You would have thought that I had slapped some of them in the face, the looks they gave me, but their were some who respected my words.

I told them what was in my heart, even though I was afraid that they would attack me. And the leader told them to let me speak, because, he said, I was telling the truth. I stayed around and talked with several of them for hours. Four of the gang members walked me home late that night.

I went to church that next Sunday. I believe it was a Pentecostal church, but I don't recall. I just remember how they made me feel. People won't remember words you say, as much as the way you make them feel when you are with them. And, they made me feel unimportant some, but some understood my speech. No one I thought will speak to me at that moment. I did not say a word. I sat in the back. Not one person approached me. Years after I have had friends who have come share good testimonies with me.

The next week I was working at Subway. I had a job lined up before I got out, at the place my brother, Danny, worked at. The manager was not patient with me, and he fired me when I couldn't get the hang of cashiering as quickly as he wanted me to.

Another attempt at a job proved to be useless. Then another, until I was wandering the streets with my friends again. The training I received in prison didn't fit well with reality. A laundryman, a dishwasher, a floor stripper; these were "proper" for prisoners.

A friend and I went to the Puerto Rican parade together. He was soon approached by several young men. I took off, a lot earlier because I didn't want any trouble that day (uncomfortable spirit) I felt the Spirit tell me to leave the area. Later that evening, I heard that he was stabbed to death.

You could see me walking on Park Street, conversing with old friends and family. You could guess, correctly, that I wasn't on my way to work.

And I was going to be a father soon. Everyone reminded me of that. Some father, hanging out with old gang buddies.

I tried going to school for a while. After high school gave me a GED, I went to college, too. There was a free grant for gang members at the music and arts school. I took acting and dancing.

I didn't get chosen for any dance routines or plays that I auditioned for until quite a few months later. By then, I was too involved in hanging around my old gang members to report to work.

I loved the worst of the gang members. He was a "brother", and my friend for many years. His name was Julio - and he was the leader of Red Alert. He was the one that let me speak. Julio was a thin-faced man with a short black beard. Being a quiet man, he listened to everyone. He was surrounded by bodyguards, who were trained to read his subtle hand gestures.

Julio was a true leader. Arrested fifty times, his longest sentence was two months. His money and connections, and good lawyers, always kept him free.

There were several policemen who also thought highly of Julio. Some of them watched him grow up. Julio had followed his dad into gang life, at the age of nine years old.

He would admit that he was afraid, at times, when he went to bed and thought about the next day. He confess this to a T.V show

Julio told me to come to the club, so he could buy me drinks. I told him, thanks, but no thanks, I was busy working on a new song that I was writing. The next thing I knew, he told all his guys to listen to my song.

"Help Tony write his song," Flamon ordered.

I was writing a rap song. In fact, I wrote quite a few of them. I was one of those young men in a wild frenzy to get into the rap business. The music business was booming in Hartford. Lots of famous rappers were coming to Hartford to perform in our clubs. Unemployment was at a steady 30 percent, so we needed to make money, and we wanted to make legitimate cash.

Park Street was in the center of Hartford, Connecticut, with major interstates running to it. It was a downtown that was rundown. That was Park Street; Dark street. That is where boys grew into men …at the age of ten…

Julio didn't need money. He needed salvation. Julio will die in prison. His sentence was life with no chance of parole. He got 13 life sentences. They sentenced him harshly for being the leader, and for every murder his members committed.

His luck just ran out. He had many prior arrests that led to nothing. He had good lawyers and lots of people who took bribes. Julio would tell you that he could never have made that kind of money legitimately. All that stopped when he went to prison. My heart is heavy when I think of him. I wanted to go visit him in prison, but I was afraid to go near that place.

I felt ashamed that I wasn't serving the Lord in any way. I wasn't talking about him, anymore, either. I stopped talking to my own family about God, too.

It has been twenty-six years since that party. I had the privilege of leading Victor Christ just before he died. We said the sinners' prayer together.

I witness strangers, as well. What joy to have had some family members next to me while we passed out tracts about salvation! When I did eventually get married, my dear x wife was also willing to join in on our street evangelism. I was also honored to have my oldest daughter Scarlet at my side.

Giving the gospel to street people is challenging, but has been the greatest experience that I have had. If we do not tell them, it would be unlikely that they would hear it anywhere else. The places that they frequent are not places you find Christians at.

Maybe that is what you are called to do. If so, you must find a safe location. The more people around, the better. If you bring a woman with you, always keep an eye on her. If you can, be located close to your church, so that you can invite them to attend a service.

Some say that scripture is the basis for the legalization of marijuana. I can say that it was a gateway drug for me. I hope this story will make some young people decide against trying it.

If you have a calling, but it is not for street gangs, the homeless, or the addicted people, it is still important. Tell whomever you are called to work with about the song in your heart. The song is "Supreme Carries Me." Rey Bendecido Amigo Fiel, Kewin Ft Rey Bendecido Eres Tu Amiga Amigo know the words, sing your own song of salvation to them.

Maybe you are called to write a book. Or, maybe you want to just start a journal. God will place things in your heart.

The church will help you discern what is of God, and what things are from Satan. The church will help point out things that you need to be doing to guard against Satan's attacks. God does not want us to be unprepared for evil. Satan has a gang after you, too.

Imagine that it is your child who had to be locked up because they were in the wrong place at the wrong time. My pastor tells the story of his youth when something similar happened to him. He was asked to get in a car with boys who were drinking. He declined. He said that decision he made kept him from getting in trouble with the police.

But things were so different for me. My pastor was not raised in my family or in my neighborhood. He was brought up in the Pentecostal church, lived with both parents, and had his grandma, (a dear saint of a woman), always close by his side. He was taught to count his blessings and fear the Lord. And he was told to stay away from bad kids. Every week church attendance, or, more often, day after day attendance, due to revivals, solidified his desire to please the Lord.

Let us say that maybe your child wasn't used to all that. Let's say that your child was trusted to make their own way in life. Let's say they got into the car when they shouldn't have. What would you do?

My advice as a parent is to check on your child. Visit them in their schools. Watch what kinds of friends they choose to be with. Keep them in church. It is easy to do if you go to church yourself.

And maybe you have. You might have been saved and sanctified by the age of five or ten, so you can't relate to this song, like I can.

AMAZING GRACE, HOW SWEET THE SOUND THAT SAVED A WRETCH LIKE ME, I ONCE WAS LOST, BUT NOW I'M FOUND, WAS BLIND, BUT NOW I SEE.

You may have escaped the wretched... or you may not have. Evil has a way of sneaking up. It slowly took over my neighborhood, my friends, and several family members that were close to me.

I was supposed to have learned that I was just a criminal, and that I would always be a criminal. I was a nobody; one who would always have a record. I would never be able to join the Marine Corps like my older brothers did. I could never vote. I was never going to be anything special to anyone. That is what prison life teaches you.

No matter what names you have been called, or what treatment you have been shown, create in yourself the person you want to be. God has made it very clear that I am special to Him. We are all special in His eyes. Tuck that inside your brain and keep it there!

Some scripture verses I read in the last year of this writing include, but are not limited to:

Matthew 19: 13-14 says, "Then were there brought unto Him little children; that he should put His hands on them, and pray: and the disciples rebuked them."

"But Jesus said, suffer little children to come unto me, for such is the kingdom of heaven."

Galatians 2:20 says, "I am crucified with Christ: nevertheless, I live: yet not I, but Christ liveth in me: and the life which I now live in the flesh I live by the faith of the Son of God, who loved me, and gave Himself for me."

2 Thessalonians 3:3 says, "But the Lord is faithful, who shall establish you, and keep you from evil."

Acts 9:15 says, "But the Lord said unto him, go thy way; for he is a chosen vessel unto me, to bear my name before the gentiles, and kings, and children of Israel."

Job 13:27 says, "Thou puttiest my feet in the stocks and stand watch over all my paths, setting a limit for the soles of my feet."

Proverbs 11:25 says, "The liberal soul shall be made fat: and he that watereth shall be watered also himself."

Galatians 6:7 says, "Be not deceived; God is not mocked: for whatsoever a man soweth, that shall he also reap."

CHAPTER THIRTEEN

Nothing but Graffiti

For as long as I live, I will never forget my gang brothers. My heart was touched by Felipe. He was the leader of the toughest gang. He was not an ordinary fighter, because he never used a gun or a weapon of any kind, but bravely fought with his bare hands.

The school said he would have made a promising football player, but he never wanted the chance to find out. He was pressured to be tough. He didn't think being in sports was tough enough. Most of his family were in and out of jail. He died fighting over a girl.

And I remember Felipe" You will see, if they haven't since painted over it, the wall where Felipe" name is emblazoned in bold red spray paint. That is all we must remember him by.

Felipe" would be a main attention grabber, cruising the streets in his car that bounced up and down. His friends were waiting on the corner for him to get them before entering a club, on the night he died. When he stepped through the crowd of people, he was stabbed in the back.

Gang life is not what it is glamorized to be. Many former members will urge you to stay out of a gang. Some of the present-day members will tell you that, too. Each dead boy, or girl, is a symbol of what gang life represents. I escaped that life before all that remained of me was a name in graffiti.

Bridgeport, Hartford and New Haven had the highest murder rates in all of Connecticut in 2003. That hasn't improved, presently in 2018, despite the city's attempt to clean it up.

I was at the hospital when my baby girl was born. She was healthy, and I planned to keep her that way. Joy was a good mother to her, and was protective. I was, too, and always made sure that no one who smoked or swore would be around my baby when I would have her for a day or two.

I was locked up for six years, and for six month after that, I wandered the streets. I didn't stand on the street corner to evangelize. I stood there trying to explain to myself and God what was wrong with me. I scolded myself for sleeping with girls out of wedlock. How could this be? I was still the one that evangelists would try to help!

I had another baby; another girl. Litza was what her mother and I named her. Oh, I wanted Litza to see me as a good father! But, at that time, I wasn't even able to see Scarlet much.

Scarlet mother didn't want me to discipline her my way, with utmost respect for the Lord and the church. I would take little Scarlet - Baby girl to church with me, only to make her sit perfectly still. I guess I was trying too hard to make both what I should have been, but failed to be, for so long.

Then there was a transformation that made me devoted, completely and forever, to His will. I was working in a Latino store just before Litza was born, and a lady (Angel) came in. She said that she wanted to speak to me, but I told her that I was the manager, not the salesman. She was insistent, telling me that it was me that she had a message for. I was getting upset with her, for I had no idea what she was, and to talk to the salesman. Talking about. She proceeded to tell me that she had a word from God. She said that I was to listen to what God wanted me to do. She was a stranger – a Christian (An anointed lady of God.)

I had already planned to go on vacation, and was just finishing up some unfinished work in the back, when she came in. I thought that this was not a good time to get a word from God. It was not clear to me until she left, that it was God's perfect timing. I cried because I knew what she said was true. I sat on the store floor and wept my heart out.

I would have scorned and mocked such a woman when I was young. But, not anymore. I knew that what she said, about me being a backslider, was a message from God. I had pulled down the shutters and turned off the light to God's word long enough. I was beginning to pass a harsh judgment against life, and sentence myself before I got all the facts. One fact, that Jesus rose from the dead, has a bearing to any judgements.

I boarded my flight for Puerto Rico. Then, I felt an angel sit near me. I could feel a presence. With wings, I was flown to the right side of Jesus.

Thought of hope

He came to me when I was hurting the most and spread His wings over me the Angel of the Lord

Six years after I was released, I was in Gurabo. With my best clothes on, I got ready for church service. It was a church service that my relative normally attended, but she couldn't go that day.

She urged me to go alone. I sat in the back, listening to the pastor, who, I felt, was speaking directly at me.

"There is someone here who needs to get the Holy Spirit," he declared. It was a Pentecostal service, and I loved it. I love gospel music, and can gospel rap for you, if you like.

I was up at the altar with new dedication in my heart. That was over twenty years ago.

I didn't stay in Puerto Rico, because a friend baby was going to be born.

When I got back to Connecticut, I stayed at a relative's house and attended their church. I never stopped going to church after that.

I went into the Goodwill with a friend recently, just to look around. We came across a coat that looked like it was made of camel's hair, or maybe goat's hair. It was a long cloak-type coat, with wide sleeves. It made me think of the coat Joseph had. As I paid for it, I joked to Roger that I hoped my church would not get jealous.

But, in all seriousness, I have been a faithful servant of God. I never have returned to a criminal life, though I did quickly return to Hartford. I lived there for more than fifteen years before moving on to a city in Georgia.

I have sent my message to other parts of the world, always testifying about His grace and mercy. In fact, I named my ministry Grace and Truth Ministries.

I started speaking in churches and halls. I told them that I made more mistakes in my life than any good I had done, so far. I told them that I had a lot of catching up to do. I had to really get God's love ingrained in my soul before I got better. And, thank God, I have gotten better.

I am not the best servant God has ever had, but I am striving to become one of them. The Best Servant Story the will of GOD. (God knows best) I have since cleared paths for many during my tenure as the senior program specialist for the Grace and Truth Ministries.

My ministry started with those on the street, but spilled over into churches I attended. I will always work with those who go to church, as well as those who don't. And, I will work with people you might be fearful of. I believe that I have been effective because I show them love. I try to show understanding. I have been where they are at. They can sense when you are afraid or disengaged. They can feel your love, though you cannot see their pain.

I thought about times when I could have been killed. If I hadn't been protected by the presence of my God, I still know God would have saved me for His purpose.

Overcrowding prisons has only strengthened prison gangs that could have led to my death. God sent His angel of protection for me there.

What is God's plan for me now, out of prison? I had been sure that there was a message from God in all that had happened. But was there a message for me, now that I was out?

YES! There was a message, and many more messages come to me each day.

Noah prepared for a disaster, just as Joseph prepared for a disaster. There will be disasters in our lives that will open doors to help others less fortunate. We can weather the storms with proper preparation. Our spiritual future needs preparation, as well.

God will lead us, and direct us to those He has chosen for us to help. The ones God chooses for you to help may be different from mine.

I thought about the tragedies that could have been avoided in my life and in the neighborhood. If only there had been more spiritual planning done!

Think about ways you can prepare for a tragedy. It should not be just for you alone that preparations should be made. We can plan ways to serve others.

You may have read about the Puerto Rican man, Joseph Badame, who stored up nonperishable food in a bunker in his home. He lived in the same house in New Jersey for many years. Inside that house were dozens and dozens of barrels of food and supplies. Each barrel weighed about three hundred pounds.

Instead of using that for a future disaster that may hit in his lifetime, he was hit by the desire to help those in Puerto Rico, who were flooded out and had no food or water in 2017.

This man did his work by preparing. Obedient to God, yet not sure of the outcome, he stored up nourishment for himself and others. The time came for him to release the bounty. Though he never imagined where this food would go, and who it would help, it helped many lives.

I want to help people, too, so I can never swerve off the narrow path again. I work wherever God wants me to work. I will sing in choirs. I will give my testimony when asked. I am directed by God, and only by God. My main love, though, is still to minister to street people.

I spend time in His word every day. I might be reading about Noah and Peter, or Paul and Moses. I am determined to learn what God wants me to know in the morning or at night. I have as much confidence in staying grounded in the Lord as I did back when I kicked out that giant motor from that van.

I married a woman who understands my passion for street evangelism. I felt an angelic presence when I sat next to her for the first time. I could sense that God was pleased with her. So, after dating for just a few months, I asked her to marry me.

My wife loves me very much, and she shows it. She is the light in a dark room. Her name is Glory, and it means Gloria in Spanish. Her presence is radiant. She is not just a candle of light in a room, but a bright sun flicked on, surging electricity and brightness into the room. I love her very much.

She speaks the truth. She is faithful and devoted to me, and she keeps a clean house. What more can a man ask for? Only one thing can I ask for, and that she loves the Lord as much as I do. And Glory does. We are equally yoked. We follow the teachings of the Bible on marriage.

Ephesians 4:15 says, "Be honest and speak truth in love."

Ephesians 4:29- 31 says, "Be forgiving."

I love to share my testimony about how God has transformed me. My life shines with a new brilliance. Yes, what more can a man ask for?

He can send His spirit to you, too, if you ask for it. I want to see you grow in knowledge of the scriptures. I want you to have such a steadfast, continual prayer life that you find it as easy as breathing. I want you to stand up when God has a calling on your life. And I want you to walk with servants that are angels in disguise.

I am walking you home.

One of the scripture verses that I read in the last twenty years have included:

John 10:27-28 says, "My sheep hear my voice, and I know them, and they follow me." Now it's your turn.

www.ingramcontent.com/pod-product-compliance
Lightning Source LLC
LaVergne TN
LVHW061039070526
838201LV00073B/5114